NvestFunds℠
Where The Best Minds Meet®

*Compliments of
Nvest Funds*

SEMINARS
THE
EMOTIONAL
DYNAMIC

Advanced Presentation Skills for Financial Professionals

---

by Frank Maselli

Published by
Creative Image
Additional copies available. Use order form in the back of this book.

Published by PowerSpeak, Inc.
Franklin, Massachusetts

Library of Congress Catalog Card Number: 96-95459

ISBN 1-57502-412-8

Additional copies may be obtained by sending a check for $27.99 (Includes shipping & handling) to the address below or by calling 800-231-5272. Visa and MasterCard are also accepted. Bulk discounts are available.

PowerSpeak, Inc.
The Art & Science of Human Communication
9 Cranberry Drive
Franklin, MA 02038
800-231-5272
www.powerspeak.com

Printed in the United States by
Morris Publishing
3212 East Highway 30
Kearney, NE 68847
1-800-650-7888

Dedicated with love to my wife

Rebecca

my eternal source of support and inspiration and the true "emotional dynamic" in my life.

Table of Contents

CHAPTER 1

A New Look at Investment Seminars

"Fortune favors the brave."
Virgil

I T TAKES GUTS TO DO SEMINARS. Investment and financial seminars have evolved into one of the most unique and demanding events in the entire realm of group communication. They require a special combination of skills ranging from detailed knowledge of a complex and ever-changing subject to advanced communication and theatrical presentation techniques. They take time, energy and effort far beyond what most advisors are willing or able to put into a disciplined business-development strategy. They also require an element of personal courage. Every time you step up to the podium, you're putting your expertise and ego on the line. Other mediums of communication are much safer by comparison.

But times have changed!

Our industry has seen a dramatic shift on several fronts including a major move away from transactions and toward relationships. This, coupled with the clients' rapidly growing desire for investment education, means the real risk to you going forward is in NOT doing seminars. Beyond that however, it's no longer enough to just "do seminars." If you're going to thrive in the new millenium...you've got to master the art.

A whole new approach
Beyond the basics

This book is a departure from anything you've seen on the subject of seminars or public speaking. We are going to take a look at seminars from the audience's perspective and explore the thoughts and emotions that are going on in their heads while you're doing the presentation. This emotion-based analysis is critical to understanding why some people become clients and others do not — why some seminars produce tremendous business results and others are a waste of time and money — why a handful of brokers and investment advisors are building huge practices with seminars while the vast majority are walking around swearing that *"%&*#@! seminars don't work!"*

We are going to consider all aspects of the seminar process — from the initial invitation to the follow-up — in the light of its effect on the audience. What emotions or feelings are produced when you say certain things in certain ways? What are they thinking about *you* while you think they're thinking something else? How do you get them to react in specific ways that lead to better message reception and better business results?

This is a big job to tackle, but we're going to have some fun doing it. When it's all over, you will be surprised at how enjoyable seminars can be and how quickly you will be able to adapt these skills and techniques to fit your own style.

Before you get too deep...
Who should be reading this book?

EVERYBODY! The principles in this book will help anyone in any field who has an opportunity to stand in front of a group of people and convince them to do something. That said, it's NOT about public speaking in general. It's a guide to one specific sub-set of the speaking universe — the investment seminar or financial presentation.

If the thought of speaking to a group of people scares you, or you have trouble putting two words together in a coherent sentence...don't read this book. It might damage you permanently. We're not going to rehash the basics like *"Don't put your hands in your pockets," "Imagine the audience in their underwear,"* or *"Bring an extra bulb for the slide projector."*

The group I've written this book for is already in the top half of one percent of the nation in public presentation ability. You are people who base your livelihood on your ability to overcome any challenge by using your mind and your mouth. Moreover, you *love* to talk. You're a group with more "ham" than a delicatessen. I could ask any one of you to deliver a five minute talk to a roomful of your colleagues on almost any subject and I'd have trouble getting you to sit down. The problem is that most of you have no formal training. This presentation ham is "uncooked." You have unbounded talent and desire with virtually no conscious competence...until now.

The people who should be reading this book include stockbrokers, financial planners, portfolio managers, investment advisors, wholesalers, insurance agents and other professionals in the financial services industry. As a group, these people spend a lot of time in front of the public, and yet they get very little coaching beyond the basics. The need for some advanced instruction is great and I hope this helps.

If you're not part of this list, that's OK. If speaking in public is a meaningful part of your life, then developing an understanding of the emotional flow within any audience can't help but make you a more potent presenter no matter what the topic. I am certain that you will pick up some very valuable speaking techniques that can be applied to any field.

Many styles but
One major goal

One of the things that make investment seminars so challenging is that they blend elements from several public speaking formats. Great seminar presenters need the conviction and charm of a politician, the empathy and persuasion of a preacher, the energy of a motivator, the knowledge and technique of a teacher, the quick wit and courage of a stand-up comic and the powerful dramatic skill of an actor. But unlike each of these other presentation mediums, seminars carry the added burden of having specific and measurable goals.

The units of measurement may be dollars as in assets under management, fees or commissions. They may also be things like community awareness, referrals or good will. Whatever yardstick you prefer, there is one basic goal of any investment seminar:

Get the audience to buy the most important product you have...YOU!

Is there any doubt in your mind that selling yourself is the most critical sale you can make? Do you understand that once an audience "buys" you...everything else falls into place? I'm hoping you share this belief. It will make things much easier as you read the rest of this book...because that's what seminars are all about.

Oh sure, seminars are educational and they teach valuable investment skills, but the real power of this medium is that seminars place you (literally and figuratively) right at center stage. You are the focus of attention, admiration, awe, contempt or disgust (depending on how you perform). There is simply no other communication modality that carries as much potential for your success as the public seminar.

Why bother with seminars?
Ask a Brontosaurus

Seminars are complex events that require lots of ability, preparation, thought and time. Why go through the hassle? You've got a million things to do and very little time to get them done. Seminars are more trouble than they're worth especially with all the other challenges that go along with managing people's money. Given all this...why bother with seminars?

According to scientists, dinosaurs were the most successful species to inhabit our planet. They ruled for tens of millions of years and were perfectly adapted to their environment. But sixty-five million years ago, a 15-mile wide meteor struck the Earth and initiated a chain of events that devastated the entire ecology. The dinosaurs, unable to adapt quickly enough, can now been seen only in museums and in movies...or in your gas tank.

In case you missed it, a meteor has struck again...this time it hit us right between the eyes.

The investment and financial services industry has undergone a tremendous upheaval over these past few years. Most of this change has been driven by a new generation of investors who are telling Wall Street that they want to do business a different way. Traditional brokerage relationships are being replaced with fee-only services.

Wirehouses are offering no-load funds. Everywhere you turn you're seeing change and the pace of this change is accelerating.

There are many causes for this change. Some might point to the Tully Commission which recommended wholesale alterations in the way brokerage firms deal with clients. Some say it's the Internet and the instant access investors have to reams of financial advice and data. To others, it's simply a matter of the Baby Boomers getting older and worrying more about their money.

Whatever the causes, it's safe to say that during the next decade and for generations to come, the business of providing financial and investment advice will be conducted in a very different way than it was just ten short years ago. This is exciting and very good news. It's also dangerous.

We must begin, right now, to incorporate new techniques and fresh ideas into our relationship-building strategies. Those who fail to modify their approach, will not only begin to lose their current clients to attrition and competition, but will be ignored by this "next generation"of investors. If we refuse to grow beyond the old ways and the methods of the past — we are destined for the same fate as befell our reptilian ancestors.

The winners in this game of business evolution will be able to answer one critical question:

What makes me different, smarter, better than my competition?

Being different and better, or being PERCEIVED as such by your client and prospect base will be your ticket to success in an ever more crowded world of financial advisors. Very few marketing tactics enable you to stand out more than seminars...especially the kind of seminars you will be doing now.

No doubt about it...
Seminars build business

Not only do seminars provide an excellent forum for exposing new investment strategies, they are a low-pressure environment for the process of client EDUCATION. This might become the single most important service element in your practice going forward. The emotional approach to seminars will make this process more efficient and effective. Your seminars will provide valuable information in an entertaining and enlightening way.

Whether you're a financial planner, an investment advisor, a stockbroker, an insurance agent or a money manager, there are two ways to grow your business. First, you can generate more business from existing clients. Second, get more clients.

The third way is to do more transactions with a client's existing assets but I caution you to avoid this. If you're busy trying to figure how to go from a commission ROA of 2.75% up to 4.0%, stop reading right now and stick your head back in the sand because you're destined for fossilization.

Seminars are the most powerful tool you have for total business development. They are the second most powerful tool for getting new clients. In this category, they lose by a nose to referrals. But the good news is that seminars actually help you get referrals.

We all love referrals. For financial professionals, there is nothing better in the world than getting regular, high-quality referrals from your existing client base. But total business development is not all prospecting. It also means servicing and educating your *existing clients*. For this broader spectrum of business needs, seminars are a clear winner.

There are three reasons for this:

1. Before you can get referrals from happy clients, you've got to have clients.

Many of you are still early in the process of building or re-building a business. You don't have a base large enough or clients comfortable enough to generate a steady stream of referrals. Oh sure, a few here and there...that's great. But enough to keep pace with attrition and to grow in real terms? Probably not yet.

2. Seminars make the referral process easier.

A strong seminar program is a fantastic way to attract the friends and colleagues of your existing clients. It is a non-threatening, educational event conducted in a comfortable, upscale and relatively anonymous setting. This is the perfect venue for being introduced to a referral and it gives them a chance to check you out while you're in top-performance mode.

Also, referrals often tend to dry up in tough market environments. Not only might you have fewer happy clients, but you may be more reluctant to ask for referrals when your clients' portfolios are declining. Seminars, being an educational tool, are just as effective, perhaps even more effective in tough times. This could keep the stream of new clients from evaporating.

3. Seminars are a tool for servicing your existing client base.

This is crucial whether or not you are actively prospecting. Maybe you're one of those fortunate few who has more clients than you can handle. If that's true, then you're not trying to grow your base, (except to counter normal attrition) but you do need to manage, service and expand the relationships you've already got. Seminars add the extra "service" dimension to your business that will form a "high-touch" communications link between you and your people. A comprehensive seminar program can also be used in conjunction with a good newsletter to accomplish the ongoing education effort.

In short...

Seminars will build your business in any kind of economic environment. You will form a bond of trust and respect between you and your clients which will make it possible to gather more of their assets and increase retention. Seminars will also position you in your community as THE person to turn to for investment advice. Ultimately, this status will have wealthy people calling you with their problems.

You'll become a "money magnet" and your biggest problem will be hiring enough support staff to manage your huge business. This is the dream goal of nearly every advisor...people calling you with money to invest. Can you believe it? Well, get ready!

Success often means taking
A new look at an old idea

Seminars are certainly not new. What's new is the way you're going to do them from now on and the results you will get. To get those results, we're going to focus on the most critical part of the entire seminar process:

What do you do with the people once they're sitting in front of you.

Most fundamental principles of public speaking remain unchanged since Caesar's day. However,

the emotion-based approach we are taking *is* new and one you're not likely to have heard from anyone anywhere.

In today's competitive world, I think it will give you an edge – a real advantage that will make you better than the competition.

Think about the seminars that are occurring in your city or town right now. If you haven't been to one, I strongly urge you to get out and see what kind of weak, low energy, confusion is being perpetrated on the investing public. The majority of advisors doing these **"Sominex Seminars"** are working by the old rules. They have no clue what the audience is feeling from one minute to the next. Consequently, they're being shunned on follow-up calls and ultimately converting only 5%-10% of attendees into clients. They're also having trouble filling the room.

By contrast, you will fill every seat and probably have to turn people away at the door. Your follow-up reception will be excellent and your client conversion rates will climb to as high as 80% or 90%! Think I'm kidding? That's the *"new look"* I'm talking about. That's what an emotion-based approach can do for you.

> *There is a growing movement in our world of financial services to understand the emotional impact of money and to help the clients not only on a basic mechanical level but on a deeper more personal level. Several groups have sprung up to address this very concept — that money is more than just numbers — it's feelings. The concepts in this book are on the cutting edge of that very positive trend.*

"But my market is seminar-ed out!"

If I had a dime for every time I've heard this one I would be writing this book from a beach in Australia. What you're really saying is that you have nothing different or better to offer. Isn't that right? Do you think McDonalds comes into a town and says *"Well, looks like no one is starving here. Let's just forget this hamburger thing."*

Sure, seminar overload is a problem. It seems that everyone who can afford to rent a room is trying their hand at public seminars. That's bad news ONLY because it provides some competition. The *good* news is that most financial seminars stink to high Heaven!

Your seminars are going to be a whole new ballgame. No more boring, uninspired amateurish lectures. Your events are going to be professional, dynamic, educational and motivational programs. Given this, I don't care if there are a dozen seminars every evening...in any market so saturated by mediocrity, there is always room for excellence. That's what you're going to be...*EXCELLENT!*

Seminars...
Not the easy road

One final thought — as much as I want to convince you to do seminars, I realize they're not for everyone. They are the road less traveled and they are more difficult than you might imagine. This book is not going to show you how easy seminars can be. If anything, it might make the process more of a challenge.

We're going to examine the tools you will need to conquer that challenge, but the decision to include seminars in your marketing and educational gameplan is based on your personality and business style. If you say *"No seminars,"* that's fine. Just be sure it's an *informed* no. But if you want to do seminars, then I say, ***"Do the best seminars you possibly can!"***

Be the absolute best in your market, your town or city. Give it 110% and not only will you reap the tremendous rewards that come with superior performance but your clients will stand a much better chance of reaching their own financial goals. And ultimately...that's what this whole ballgame is all about!

Growing your practice is getting tougher
So must you

Even with the overwhelming amount of money pouring into financial investments, the day-to-day business of growing your asset/client base has never been more difficult. Competition among banks, discounters and other full-service firms is ferocious. The complexity of the investment world has grown exponentially and clients are bombarded by vast amounts of investment information and misinformation leading to confusion, uncertainty, bad decisions and horrendous performance.

On top of that, many investors, particularly the Baby Boomer children of your best clients, think they don't need you. They're being told by the popular media that to use a full-service broker or to pay a fee for professional investment advice is a waste of time and money. We know this is shortsighted and wrong, but convincing them is not always an easy job.

Think I'm wrong? Just wait until you have that inevitable conversation with the 45-year old son or daughter of your best trading account. It will go something like this:

YOU

Tom, I'm very sorry to hear about your Dad. He was a friend and a client for twenty years and I will miss him tremendously.

Baby Boomer Child of Top Client

Thanks, Frank. It's nice of you to say that. Dad always spoke very highly of you. Oh, by the way, when can I pick up the check?

YOU

(bewildered) What check?

Baby Boomer Child of Top Client

Well, I've decided to close out the account.

YOU

(stunned and fumbling) Before you do that, why don't we get together to discuss the portfolio. There are some positions you might want to hold on to. I've managed this money for twenty years and we've done pretty well. I'd hate to see you make a hasty decision.

Baby Boomer Child of Top Client

Thanks, but I've given this a lot of thought. I've been doing no-loads and I read Money Magazine pretty thoroughly. Plus I'm on the Internet now and

> I just can't imagine that I'd need a financial advisor.
> I'll be in at 2:00 to pick up the check.
>
> ### *YOU*
>
> *(helpless and defeated)* Well, we've got to liquidate the stocks...it will take three days at least to get you a check.
>
> ### *Baby Boomer Child of Top Client*
>
> Three days, huh? OK, then forget the stocks, just transfer the entire account to MegaDiscount Superbroker. I have the number right here.

Bang...you're dead! Call me when this happens to you. You'll need a shoulder to cry on.

Seminars may not be able to prevent this scenario in all cases, but they will tilt the balance back to your favor. You are more likely to build a solid relationship with the next generation of investors through direct, face-to-face contact. A seminar allows you to provide the education they're demanding AND sell yourself at the same time. This transmission of "wisdom" helps keep the assets in place.

In focus groups all across the country, the investing public is telling Wall Street to stop selling and start educating. They want to know a lot more than simply what to buy — they want to know why a strategy makes sense, what's the long-term game plan, how the portfolio works in terms of both risk and return. They want solutions to their problems not products. They want and need more than they've been given, and there are only two people who can give it to them — you or your competition. Who is it going to be?

The kind of seminars you will be doing after you read this book will be high-content, enjoyable events with no sales pressure. This is precisely what investors want. In fact, your seminars will exceed most audiences expectations by a wide margin because you're going to do things they've never seen done in any investment seminars. In short — you're going to blow them away!

"Ms. Jones, call on line 2...it's Just another stockbroker!"

If you work for a major investment firm, brokerage house, mutual fund or insurance company, chances are that the average investor has no clue who you are and why you're different from any other firm. There are a few notable exceptions to this — companies that have carved out a specific niche in the public's mind. But most investors think of this business as one gigantic ocean of financial information. If you're part of this industry, the need for you to differentiate yourself from the crowd has never been greater than it is today.

If you're independent, you might actually have it worse in some ways. Even if your message is totally unique, your performance is exceptional and your service is *extra-terrestrial*...the lack of capital means your marketing reach is limited. Chances are you're reaching a small piece of your potential audience.

This may not be happy news, and I'm not trying to make you mad. All I want is to help you understand the need to stand out. I've always operated by three rules.

1. If you're not growing...you're liquidating.

2. If you're not wired *(computerized)*...you're retired.

3. If you're not different...you're dying.

Number three is the key here. As a medium of communication, seminars afford you the best opportunity to distinguish yourself from your competition. Whether you use them as a full-time element of your marketing strategy or only as periodic special events, they can generate tremendous results. No other form of contact allows you to display such a broad variety of skills and knowledge. You have a chance to really shine and impress people — to be witty, intelligent, charming, dynamic and caring all at the same time.

I said I wasn't trying to convince you to do seminars, but I'm doing a good imitation. One more argument and then I'll shut up.

Don't take my word for it...
Do the math

As a young stockbroker, I was taught that building my business was "a numbers game." If I heard that once I heard it a million times. In reality, it *is* a numbers game. But instead of dials and contacts, we need to look at different numbers.

Raise your hand if you are actively cold calling. Anyone? (I actually heard an ad on the radio this morning about a sales training workshop in cold calling. It's coming back into vogue...can you imagine?) Well, chances are you're NOT cold calling anymore, but you might have an intern or group of telemarketers working for you. In either case, consider a few statistics. Add up all the contacts you make and the amount of real conversation time you spend with each contact on a cold call or a follow-up. You might be shocked to know how little actual communicating you're really doing.

I knew one broker who busted his butt on the phone every day. He called himself the Cold Call Cowboy *(Very original! How many Cold Call Cowboys were there in the 80s?)* This fellow calculated that he spent an average of forty seconds talking to thirty contacts each day. That's a lot of contacts — six hundred contacts per month. This equals roughly twenty actual "prospect-minutes" a day times twenty days equals 400 prospect-minutes (6.7 hours) a month.

Compare that to a seminar.

Call for the same 20 days on your seminar and talk to 30 people each day. That's still 600 people you've reached. Say only ten percent of them confirm and half of that group shows up for the seminar. That's thirty people in the room for sixty minutes. That comes out to 1,800 prospect minutes versus 400 from aggressive cold calling.

Here you see a fundamental difference between the old "numbers game" and the "quality game."

I could make the subjective case that calling to invite people to an educational meeting is much less threatening and stressful than trying to sell a stranger something over the phone. Thus you will enjoy it more and therefore be able to make more calls in the same amount of time. But forget the subjective case for a minute.

Why would you do the same thing that fast talking investment salespeople have been doing since money was invented — something which the clients have repeatedly said they hate and have passed legislation to outlaw— something which gives an investor less than a minute to make an important decision about their financial future — something which gives you virtually no chance to sell yourself or explain how your investment idea fits into a complex financial environment — something which shows the least unique side of your abilities and makes you appear as a common huckster to be rushed off the phone...

...are you nuts?

Was that a leading question?

Seminars will not only be more fun for you but the quality of your message can improve dramatically. There's a heck of a lot more probing, educating, informing and value adding you can do in sixty uninterrupted minutes with a roomful of prospects than you can in forty seconds with each one individually!

Which leads us to another major revelation — the reason seminars are better than almost anything else is the...

Little understood principal of...
The group dynamic

Whenever you put two or more people together in a room something happens. They stop being individuals and they become part of this vague social structure called a group. Their behavior changes in subtle and sometimes dramatic ways.

One obvious shift is that they become much more aware and attuned to the reactions of people around them. They begin to react to you based not only on their own impulses but on their perception of the other people's reactions. They will check themselves in the mirror of the crowd to judge the appropriateness of their reactions.

If others are laughing, they will laugh. If others are smiling and nodding, they will smile and nod. If others are feeling good and positive and enthusiastic about you, they will feel the same way. It works like a charm and it cannot be duplicated in any venue other than with a roomful of people. By understanding and tapping into the emotional flow that's controlling this behavior, you can influence not only individuals, but the bulk of an audience all at once!

I'm simplifying this quite a bit for our discussion here. There are many aspects to a group dynamic that have been studied by experts for decades. You should also know that the group dynamic isn't cast in stone nor does it always work to your benefit. For example, if people see others looking bored and eager to leave, they will begin to feel bored as well. If someone feels confused, they will check to see if others look confused and if so, they will begin to feel more confused and annoyed at you for confusing them.

There are also some people who may consciously or unconsciously react in the opposite manner as they perceive others reacting. So you may think you're doing a great job in front of a room but you'll notice one guy off in the corner frowning and shaking his head when others are smiling and nodding theirs.

Soon, he may begin to influence others around him and you will witness the formation of a sub-space warp bubble through which your charm, wit and intelligence cannot penetrate. This is very rare but it does happen.

Recognizing and managing the group dynamic will help you sell yourself with tremendous synergy. You will be able to compound good feelings. Your use of humor will be more effective. Each emotional state you reach will have a greater impact and the effect will be extremely rewarding. A solid understanding of this dynamic will also help you avoid those rare moments when it's working against you and you'll be able to nip them in the bud.

"But Frank...
Do seminars really work?"

This is the basic question everyone asks all the time, but it's the wrong question to ask. Of course seminars work. They work well in nearly every economic environment and throughout each market cycle. They work in cities, suburbs and rural country towns. They work morning, noon and night on every day of the week including Sundays. They work with novice investors as well as experienced stock and bond traders. They work — period!

But like any tool, seminars are only as good as the craftsman. After fifteen years in this business it has been my observation that very few financial professionals know how to do a really good seminar. I've been to hundreds of seminars and I can only think of a dozen or so that moved an audience to any significant degree. That's a pretty dismal statistic.

And this isn't your basic bell-shaped curve here. I would estimate that fully seventy percent of the seminars I've seen have been terrible — really bad — the kind that make you want to get up, walk out and hide your money under a rock. My guess is that's exactly what the audience did too. These are seminars that did NOT work...a tool mishandled by an unskilled craftsman. They wasted time, space and effort, but generated no positive results for either the presenter or the audience.

And I'm not a harsh critic. In fact, I'm the world's greatest audience! I'm one of those people who really roots for the speaker to do a great job. I smile and laugh at all the right moments. I ask great leading questions. I'm the perfect shill. And still I've been completely shocked at the low quality of these presentations.

It concerns me that major financial and securities firms could allow one of their representatives to get up in front of a roomful of existing or potential clients and deliver a weak message and poor image. Quality control in a public presentation environment is a life and death necessity. As far as I can see, it's lacking.

The problems I've seen range across an entire spectrum of bad public speaking techniques including fundamental deficiencies like poor grammar, low energy, lack of preparation, unreadable visual aids, mistyped handouts and a very uncomfortable environment. Most of these seminars were deathly boring. I'm talking snore city! Some were too thin in factual content, others too heavy. Most were badly organized and hard to follow from premise to conclusion to call-to-action. Some were so confusing that I actually thought I was in the wrong room. One seminar, I will never forget, was such a high-pressure sales event that it felt as if some giant unseen electronic force had locked onto the magnetic strips of all my credit cards and was pulling my wallet right out of my pocket.

Hey, wait a minute...
My seminars are great!

You may be part of that elite corps of financial professionals who really knows what to do in front of a room. Maybe you're already giving top-quality, emotion-packed, value-added seminars. If so, I salute you. Keep it up. You're on your way to tremendous success (if you're not there already). The only suggestion I can make is: Don't get complacent! I urge you to keep training and expanding your skills. Even the best public speakers have to freshen their material and sharpen their delivery from time to time or they risk going stale.

But for the rest of you who are not yet great — you can be. All it takes is some knowledge, training and a bit of creative flair or personality. Please don't think any of this is beyond you. Some people are going to be naturally better at it than others, at first, but everything in this book is learnable. If I can do it *(well, that's a bad example since I am exceptionally gifted)* but you get the idea. No one is born a fantastic speaker. The vast majority of top presenters are self-made with little or no formal education. Now you've got an edge, a coach if you will. So read on!

> *By the way. If you ARE really good at seminars, I'd love to hear from you. We're forming a seminar chapter on the Internet as part of my firm's web site at **www.mutualfunds.com**. We will be publishing ideas from around the country including a section entitled **"How Would You Do It?"** where we address specific seminar-related problems. Not only is it nice to hear from people who share your interests and concerns, but you might pick up a trick or two that makes your next seminar a smash! So tune in and contribute. Your insights would be very valuable to the group. E-Mail is fmaselli@mutualfunds.com.*

No theoretical nonsense, only
Real-world insights

The entire emotion-based approach may seem very new or advanced, but nothing you will read in here is theory. I've done all of it in a public seminar forum. There are no clever "paper concepts." All of it has been proven in the field under a variety of stressful and difficult circumstances.

Initially, you may be quite uncomfortable with many of the things we're going to discuss. That's OK. Give yourself time. I'm asking you to think in a new way. That's not easy. Some of these techniques may seem strange or too difficult to try. That's OK too. Even if you pick up one thing, one idea or tool you can use, you will see positive results almost immediately. That feedback will compel you to speak more often and thus quicken your advance.

The ideas you will read here come from three primary sources:

- Six years of extensive research into the field of interpersonal communications.
- Direct observation and study of hundreds of public speakers and presentations.

- The personal experience of having done over 1,000 seminars as well as 25 years of public speaking and theatrical stage work.

Over time, you will be able to modify and perfect these techniques to fit your specific needs and personality. These skills will make your seminars, however strong they may be right now, more powerful — the result being more smart, happy clients, and more business!

CHAPTER 2

What Makes a Great Seminar?

"It is a rough road that leads to the heights of greatness."
Lucius Annaeus Seneca

"Greatness knows itself."
Shakespeare

B efore we go further, it might help to determine what constitutes a seminar. I define a "seminar" as any presentation made to a group of people. This leaves lots of room for variation in size or format. You may be the only speaker, you may be part of a group of presenters or you may be hosting a guest such as a portfolio manager, wholesaler or research analyst. The group may have come specifically to see you, or you may be a guest speaker at an organization such as the Rotary, Kiwanis or Lions Club.

The seminar may be a ten-minute presentation to a pension committee or a 20-hour, multi-week adult education course at the local community college. It might also be a tele-seminar conducted over a phone line, (although much of what we'll be discussing in this book is only useful in a face-to-face scenario). Basically, anytime you're speaking to two or more people — you're giving a seminar.

You could make the case that *any* sales presentation is a form of seminar. Audience size has little bearing on the fundamentals of good presentations. However, the skills you will learn in this book will be most helpful with groups ranging anywhere from five to five hundred people. A great deal of these skills will also help you with one-on-one presentations, or a "micro-seminar."

Some of you may find that they even add new life to your one-on-one telephone conversations as well. It's all one unified field out there — the skills are identical with only marginal variation for the venue.

What makes a seminar great?

Being results-oriented, most financial advisors would say that the ultimate measure of a successful seminar is the amount of business done as a direct result of the event. I believe that this definition is too narrow and could lead to a fatal myopia in your marketing strategy.

A seminar is not only a fee- or commission-generating tool. It's a critical step in the continuous process of building trusting relationships with both prospects and clients.

Don't get me wrong. In nearly all cases, a good seminar will generate business right away. But some investors may not yet be ready to make a move. By no means does that mean you've failed. Instead, we need to broaden the measure of a "good" seminar to include other things.

By the way, if you have to deal with a branch manager or a supervisor of some sort, don't let them judge your seminars by the gross fees or commissions either. Be sure they understand that this is a long-term commitment on your part and that you expect them to be your partner in this effort.

This is especially true if you're just starting out. It may take three or four seminars before you drop a single ticket. Both you and your manager need to be prepared to stay the course, even if revenue dollars are not an immediate result. The gross, the fees, the assets, the new accounts and the success will all come if you stick to your game plan.

No manager worth his/her salt will ever refuse to support a well-thought-out business plan implemented with enthusiasm.

Quite the contrary. They want to see you succeed and they want to help. That's what hits *their* hot button. It was just such a proactive and insightful branch manager at Dean Witter in Baltimore who got me started down this seminar path as a rookie broker. He saw that I hated to cold call and that my numbers were weak despite having significant raw sales talent. I'll never forget what he told me...

"Frank, I don't care how you build your business...as long as it's legal. (Hey this was the eighties!) I want to help you build it any way that makes you happy. If you do something you're good at and that you enjoy doing it...you're going to do more of it and you'll be a tremendous success!"

His words stuck with me, and I've lived by them ever since. So a good manager can be a boon to your success. Avail yourself of their skill and experience whenever you can. If you are just getting started or you feel that you need some help developing a seminar gameplan...call me. I can help you design a program that you'll be able to " sell" to any manager.

The mark of a great seminar

I judge a successful seminar by several measures including:

- ### APPOINTMENTS

Appointments are a direct payoff of a great seminar. You use the seminar event to create interest in a concept and credibility in yourself. Then you follow-up with a personal appointment at which you may probe and profile more deeply or actually invest the assets for a qualified client or prospect.

I will typically measure success by the number of appointments set within four weeks of the event. This four-week time frame is not arbitrary. Experience has shown that beyond the four week mark the prospects have cooled off to the point where the memory of the seminar alone is usually not sufficient to bring them in for an appointment. You will need to re-light the fire in them. Keep in mind that the cool-off time for an *ordinary* seminar tends to be much shorter than for one of your SUPER-seminars. An average seminar may see people cooling by the time they reach the parking lot. Four weeks assumes you're doing some good work up there.

At some point you will get good enough and your seminars will become so powerful that people who attended seminars months or even years ago will convert to clients. Imagine someone calling you out of the blue,

> **"You may not remember me but I came to your seminar last year. My advisor just retired and I was wondering if you had some time to meet with me."**

It happens, believe it. It's a powerful feeling that will bring a tiny tear to your eye. People change, and so do their relationships with financial advisors. If you've placed yourself in their minds as a value-added professional who knows his stuff, when change does come, they will remember you.

• REFERRALS

Here's the scenario: an existing client attends your seminar. This client has not been a source of referrals thus far in your relationship but after the seminar she suggests that you call her friend or she fills out three or four names on your next client referral letter. This is a major success!

> *Just so you know...there is a very strong emotional undercurrent to the process of getting referrals. It could be the subject of another book. By using the emotion-based techniques during your seminars, you will have paved the way for those referrals and the flow will come much easier.*

Or how about this? One of the seminar attendees was so impressed by your presentation that he invites you to speak to his company's investment club or their pre-retiree group or his Elks Lodge. Here the referral is another seminar and another chance to reach new clients. The effect can begin to snowball.

> *During every seminar, you should mention that you are available for special speaking engagements or as an "emergency speaker" to fill in on short notice in case they have a cancellation. If anyone in the audience is a member of an organization, club, company, or any other group that might be interested in a similar presentation or a customized event, you would be happy to visit them. You might even want to include your "Menu" in the handout kit.*
>
> *This menu is a listing of topics on which you can speak. It doesn't need to be too elaborate, but it should contain some exciting and thought-provoking*

titles with a brief description of each seminar including the approximate time you need. See Appendix.

- ## PUBLIC & GROUP AWARENESS

Let's assume that you're prospecting in a small to medium-sized town or in a local retirement community. You're doing a seminar but you're also cold calling and mass mailing to get business. This is part of a strategy called "farming" an area where you use a multi-layered marketing strategy to penetrate a region. The local newspaper or community newsletter carries a story about your seminar. (A story that you submitted as a press release.) This could be a very powerful aid to your "farming" effort. Not only will some people recognize your name from the article but you can include copies in any mailings you may do and refer to the event and the article during any cold calls.

The key to remember is that public awareness doesn't just happen...you are in control and must *make* it happen. Your seminar is an important event but you've got to make it easy for the local media to help you by sending press releases, biographies, announcements, photos, etc. Naturally, this works better in smaller communities, but there's no reason you can't divide a major metropolitan area into smaller sub-sets for "farming" purposes.

Group awareness is also a major benefit of seminars. Let's say your target market is printers. You speak at the New Jersey Printers Association meeting and *The Printing News* carries a story about you in their next issue. This becomes a strong connection when you talk to other printers. If they missed the story you can send it to them. It says you're an insider, you're one of them. Your receptivity within the group goes through the roof. You get invited to their national conference. You get on their advisory board. You write a special investing column for their monthly newsletter. Eventually, everyone in that group knows who you are and what you do.

- ## STATURE IN THE COMMUNITY

How would you like to be the advisor to whom everyone in your community with serious money turns to for help and advice? Seminars are the way. If this is your goal, you're probably going to need to do a regular, on-going series of events. One way is to teach an Adult Education class.

For two years I taught a seminar on investing at the local community college. Nothing special here...many brokers have done this. What I did, however, was slightly different with dramatically improved results. I looked through the college course catalog and saw that all the basic courses were taken by other instructors, so I changed tactics. The title of my course was **"Advanced Investment Techniques."** I advertised it in the catalog by saying *"This is the course your broker doesn't want you to attend!"*

I effectively declared to the community that I was superior, I was the expert ABOVE the other instructors. I teach the *"graduate"* course. People with *"serious money"* come to my course. I'm different, smarter and better than all the other brokers.

Did I frighten some people away? Sure. But did I get a better group with bigger assets bases? You bet your life! One poor fellow had just been thrust into a new job as the pension manager for a major regional firm with $260 million in assets. He needed help, but **"Fundamentals of Investing"** just wasn't the ticket. Even though I didn't get the pension account, I did get several personal accounts of key people in the company based on my relationship with him.

Whenever I talked to anyone in the community during my other prospecting efforts, I mentioned that I taught *"the advanced course"* at the college. This carried added weight and led to significant business that would never have otherwise come my way.

• ELEVATED RELATIONSHIPS

Let's say that you've done a little business with a particularly tough new client. Maybe she's done a couple of trades or has given you a little money to "test you out." She's always seemed a little resistant to your ideas or your approach and reluctant to open up. Suddenly, after the seminar, she is more responsive to your probes about her financial needs and agrees to a one-on-one meeting.

I'd call that a huge victory! Here, the seminar has helped elevate the quality of the relationship and brought this client closer to you. It has helped you *"mine the gold"* in your own book!

• PERSONAL ENJOYMENT

This could very well be the single most important reason for doing seminars. Perhaps you're the kind of person who gets a thrill out of standing up in front of a roomful of strangers and holding them spellbound for an hour. Imagine being the center of attention with the power to positively influence people's financial lives merely by the force of your convictions and the impact of your delivery. Make no mistake — the roar of the crowd is a powerful intoxicant. Tapping into this excitement can kick your business into high gear. You may have the potential to surpass even your wildest expectations.

A great seminar is a lot more than
A packed house

Ask 100 advisors and 99 of them will tell you that the most important part of doing a seminar is *"getting people to come."*

WRONG!

Certainly, generating attendance is important, and we've got an entire chapter devoted to it, but it's trivial compared with the event itself. Getting people to attend is simply a matter of effort. Creativity has some part to play, but most of us have to go through some compliance process with your written invitations. By definition, compliance is the opposite of creativity. If you do the work, they will come; if not, they won't. Filling a room is only one percent of the job.

Generating attendance is a simple, 5-step process that anyone can follow. The key (I will tell you now so you don't panic and rush to Chapter 17) is to sell the seminar itself with as much intelligence and enthusiasm as you would a prime growth stock. Talk about the benefits of attending – how they will be smarter or somehow better-off for taking the time to come hear you. Talk about the timeliness of the topic, the excitement it is generating among investors. Refer to recent articles or third party mentions of the topic.

Make them feel that by coming to your seminar they are special in some way. Don't underestimate the importance of this sale. It should be as well-thought-out as any investment presentation you could make.

If you use cold-callers to do your seminar prospecting, they need to be carefully schooled in what can and cannot be said. There are compliance restrictions on any cold-call script, however, no one says they can't use a little energy and enthusiasm as well. But remember — a standing room only crowd is meaningless unless you're able to do something with them.

By far, the most critical part of the entire seminar process happens once they sit down and you start talking. That's when the audience starts on the psychological journey from *Mildly Interested Stranger* to *Client-for-Life*. What you say and how you say it for the next 45 - 90 minutes will determine the ultimate success or failure of your entire seminar effort.

I can't tell you how many times I've been in the audience of standing-room-only seminars filled with intelligent investors only to see that tremendous potential wasted by a speaker who was unprepared, untrained or unconscious.

When they walk out of YOUR seminar, they will be abuzz with energy and enthusiasm. You will have gained a measure of prestige in their minds that no other advisor can match. You will have set ten appointments right there. You will have people asking you to speak at their clubs or company retirement groups. Those who are ready to invest will want your help. Those who aren't ready yet will magnetize your name to the giant refrigerator door in their minds for ready reference. They will warmly welcome your follow-up calls and and you will be the first one *they* call when they are ready

What are you going to say?
It helps to have a topic

I'm assuming that you have something to say. There are three main sources for seminar material.

First is your own company. Many of you may work for a major investment firm all of whom have some sort of pre-packaged public seminars including slides or overheads. The benefit of these is that they are usually pretty slick and well-designed by a marketing department. Also, they're probably pre-approved by Compliance. The drawback is that they look very slick and well-designed by a marketing department. They do not usually look like thoughts coming out of your own head. This is important for reasons we'll discuss later.

Second, you could buy a complete seminar package including slides, handouts and invitations from one of several companies that specialize in the seminar marketing business. One you may have heard of is *"Successful Money Management Seminars"* out of Colorado. These are solid presentations, but they're pretty expensive. Buying and maintaining the seminar can cost thousands! But here again, the issue is mental ownership of the words and ideas. *Although for $10,000 I can convince myself that I wrote the Gettysburg Address.*

The third and best source for seminar material is your own brain.

To be truly powerful and effective I believe you have to create your own seminar. The difference is like an actor speaking the words written by a long-dead author. They may be great words, but everyone knows you're acting.

Creating a seminar may sound like a daunting task, but it's really a lot of fun. We'll talk more about this in Chapter 5, but it's more a matter of organization and clever borrowing. Once you know the basic theme, you break it down into bite-sized chunks and begin collecting ideas from a diverse group of sources including wholesalers, product marketing materials, industry publications, news media, books, articles, other speakers, portfolio managers, analysts, economists, etc. This involves cutting out articles, scanning important magazines and wire stories for facts, quotes and statistics — developing what I call a seminar *"story book."* There is no industry that fills your brain, desktop and wastebasket with more information than financial services. You will never starve from lack of ideas or data in this business.

This act of creating your own seminar leads to another, equally critical benefit of doing seminars — you will become a much smarter, more capable professional than your colleagues or competition. Why? Because you not only have to know lots of "stuff" but you have to know it well enough to TEACH OTHERS! That carries a massive added responsibility which many people shun. Embracing this responsibility will set you above the crowd and dramatically improve the quantity, quality and enjoyment of your business.

CHAPTER 3

Emotional, Not Logical

"Emotion is the chief source of all becoming-conscious. There can be no transforming of darkness into light and of apathy into movement without emotion."

Carl Gustav Jung

THE ESSENCE OF A SUPER-SUCCESSFUL seminar...is your ability to create and control a specific pattern of emotions in the minds of the audience. It is these emotions that will move them to action, not logic, not statistics, not facts, not great investment ideas (although all of these are used in the process).

A super seminar becomes an emotional train-ride where you are the conductor with a firm hand on the throttle. You are in control and through your skill they will experience the range of emotions including fear, confusion, anger, joy, enthusiasm, relief and excitement.

The ability to create a specified set of emotions in an audience of virtual strangers and, simply by the power of your message, motivate them to take decisive action, may be the highest level of human communication. This is especially true when dealing with people's money. It's a set of skills that can be attained only through proper training and experience.

In the following chapters I will break the seminar process down into the emotional building blocks that underpin the entire communication process. Then we will go into greater depth with each emotional condition and how you get there. When we're done, we will have carefully reviewed every major aspect of the seminar process from the invitation to the follow-up. You will be thoroughly prepared to solo.

The reason we're doing it this way is that the emotions will give you the reasons for doing what you must do. Actors call it the "motivation." If you understand the emotional goal, you will transcend the simple rote memorization of presentation chronology. You will begin to react creatively and with intuition. THAT'S...when things will start to really happen for you!

Here's a brief
Emotional overview

As you stand in front of the audience, how do you want people to feel? What combination of emotions do you want flowing around in their heads throughout the event? How can you create and control these emotions to maximize the business and relationship potential of the seminar?

I've developed an acronym for this set of emotions that should help stimulate your memory. The acronym is named after one of our society's great communicators — a man who rarely spoke an intelligible word but who could convey more emotional content with a grunt or facial gesture than a Greek chorus. The man was Lurch — from The Addams Family — the old television sitcom with Gomez and Morticia and Uncle Fester. Lurch was the silent towering butler (played by Ted Cassidy) who's famous line was *"You rang?"*

The acronym is **LURCH FACE**. Sounds crazy? Maybe. But from now on you won't be able to forget it. We will go into each of these in much greater detail but here is a brief overview.

L — LIKE
Most critically, you want the audience to like you as a person on an instinctive, "gut" level. People do business with people they like. That's an accepted axiom of the sales profession and it should be the primary overt and covert goal of your seminar. If you achieve none of the other emotional objectives, getting prospects to like you will

still leave you with a chance to follow-up and get them in for an appointment.

U — UNDERSTANDING

You want them to have a clear understanding of your message without distortion or confusion. There's nothing better than when someone comes up to you after the seminar and says how clear and understandable you made everything. You've gone a step toward de-mystifying the world of money and you must be really smart to do that (or so they'll think!).

R — RESPECT

You want them to have respect for you as a professional who knows the intricacies of the investment world and can solve their problems.

C — CONFIDENCE

You want them to feel confident in your abilities, knowledge and judgment and have a sense that you are an expert. You want them to trust that you have their best interests in mind. You also want them to have greater confidence in their own decision-making ability.

H — HAPPY

You want them to feel happy about themselves for having taken the time to come to your seminar and you want to create an air of happiness and fun throughout the event. You also want to use humor where appropriate to stimulate memory, relax the audience and build rapport.

F — FEAR

You want them to feel fear in sufficient quantity and emotional intensity to get them questioning themselves about their own financial future. You don't want them to feel gloomy or depressed, but feelings of directed discontent are crucial to prompt a prospect to work with you. If all you did was cheer them up and make them feel great about what they're currently doing, where is their motivation to call YOU for an appointment?

A — ACTION

You must outline and gain agreement on specific **action** steps as a solution to their problem AND you must motivate them to actually do something! Getting someone to do something is a very emotional process. Inertia is a comfortable state that is hard to break out of. Make it easy for them by doing all the emotional "machete work."

C — CHANGE

They must recognize the need for change in their present situation and they must know that change is a normal and healthy part of any investment strategy. Ideally, they will embrace and come to enjoy change.

E — EXCITEMENT / ENERGY / ENTHUSIASM

These are three "E"-emotions that all tie together to make a fantastic presentation. You want them to feel all three by the time you're done. This will enhance your message and your ability to help them reach their goals.

L - Like

U - Understanding

R - Respect

C - Confidence

H - Happy

F - Fear

A - Action

C - Change

E - Excitement

The sum of these emotions is embodied almost totally in one word:

— TRUST —

At the end of your seminar, the people should walk out believing they can trust you to be an expert in your field, to deliver on your promises, to put forth a maximum effort on their behalf and to always act in their best interests.

Trust, however, is too big to understand. It's one of those multi-faceted emotions that involves liking, respect, confidence and all the others mentioned above. I highlight it because it's the one word clients most often use to describe their own emotional state. You need to be aware of it as the defining condition and objective in their minds. During the entire seminar process they will assay their feelings about you and come to an emotional decision – *"I trust him"* or *"I don't trust him."* There is only one good outcome.

Now the question becomes, ***"How do you create this state of mind in the audience?"*** It's time to get into the nine emotional steps. Let's examine in detail, some of the specific emotion-evoking mechanisms that you can use in your next seminar.

CHAPTER 4

LIKE

"People do business with people they like."
Anonymous

I DON'T KNOW WHO SAID IT FIRST...but there are few truer words in the world of sales and no more critical goal of a public presentation.

You may not be the smartest or best financial advisor in town. You may not even have done a particularly good seminar. Let's go so far as to say that you completely failed to achieve every other emotional condition in this book. But, for some strange reason, the audience walks out feeling as though they like you — you will STILL see very positive results from the event. You will still have a chance to connect on a deeper, more personal level. They will take your call and even agree to an appointment.

If they DON'T like you...well it's like Dr. McCoy said to Captain Kirk —

"He's DEAD Jim!"

They will find some reason on a conscious or sub-conscious level to NOT do business with you.

Getting the audience to like you is a process that flows through the entire seminar. It permeates every aspect of your presentation and involves the organization of the event, the nature of the content, the energy and enthusiasm you display, the general tone of your voice, the use of humor and a whole list of other variables. But the interesting thing to note is that liking starts long before you ever say a word or before the event begins. It starts with the one variable that reaches an audience first.

Make it exciting and fun...
The Invitation

Your seminar invitation is the initial contact you make with your potential audience. It has to do a big job. I'm assuming, by the way, that you're using a written invitation of some kind. Any serious seminar will have a written invitation. You may use the phone to follow-up, but some kind of physical document is essential.

The invitation must provide all the critical facts about the seminar in an easy-to-find format with no ambiguity. Items like time, date, location and RSVP instructions should be immediately visible. You must make it as easy as possible for people to respond. But this is obvious. Let's dig deeper.

The topic title should be interesting and catchy if possible. I say "if possible" because much of your written material may require approval by Compliance and that can be a limiting factor in your creative effort. But where you have some editorial leeway, try to find an interesting and entertaining way of saying what you've got to say.

I'm no advertising copywriter, but here are some examples of possible ways to say the same thing. These are only my suggestions, you may have many more ideas...so use them.

Typical: Saving For Retirement
Option 1:   America's Retirement Crisis & Five Ways to Avoid It
Option 2:   Retirement Peace of Mind — How to Get it & Keep It
Option 3:   Sorry, You're Out of Money!

Typical: Stock Market Investing
Option 1:   7 Secrets of Highly Profitable Investors
Option 2:   Dow Jones 10,000 — What It Can Mean for You
Option 3:   Bull or Bear - What's Next for Stocks & Why?

Typical: Reduce Your Income Taxes
Option 1:   Taxes Hurt...Please Stop the Pain!
Option 2:   22 Ways to Save on Income Taxes...RIGHT NOW!
Option 3:   How to Say "No" to Uncle Sam & Survive

These may not be the best ideas for headlines but the key is to catch their interest fairly quickly. I don't think you can expect people to wade through paragraphs of stuff to get excited about a seminar.

I use bullet points, call-outs, shading and a host of other graphic techniques to make my invitation exciting and interesting. Don't go too crazy with graphics and fancy design or you run the risk of looking unprofessional. A simple $8^1/_2$ x 11 page folded in thirds with the guts on the front and some endorsements on the back. (See Appendix)

Also, take care not to look too home grown. I've seen invitations that looked like they were done on a 1950's mimeograph machine. We live in a computerized age and people have come to expect a certain look to the printed material they receive. That includes laser printing as opposed to typing, dot matrix or crayon. Yes, being different and a little retro can often be a marketing benefit — but not if your invitation is unreadable.

Endorsements

People love endorsements! If you think of a seminar as being similar to a movie or a play you will understand what I'm about to suggest. When you read a movie review in the newspaper and you see *"Two Thumbs Up!"* from Siskel & Ebert, or *"A Blockbuster Smash Hit!"* from the New York Times, what goes through your mind? Chances are you may be a little more excited about seeing that movie. This is a well known fact — people like to see that they are making a decision that others have already made and enjoyed. It's human nature. So why not use this to your advantage.

On your invitation, why not include quotes from happy past attendees like:

"The most fun I've had in years."

"This was a highly stimulating and enlightening evening."

"I've been to seven seminars this year and yours was better than all of them put together!"

"Totally enjoyable...and no sales hype!"

These are actual written comments I've received from my own public seminars over the years. I've included them in subsequent seminar invitations. You can get comments simply by asking for them and handing out a critique sheet at the end of the seminar. I will even go so far as to joke with my audience and say,

"On your seminar invitation, you may have noticed some endorsements from past seminars. I just want you to know that you too can have your name immortalized on all my future invitations if you use the appropriate amount of enthusiasm and hyperbole on your critique sheet. And if you have nothing nice to say...I need to hear that too. I really put a lot of effort into these seminars and your feedback is absolutely vital to me...so please fill out the critique sheet."

Sure, it's a half-joke, but the message is clear. I want endorsements and I'm not too proud to ask for them. Every now and then you will run across someone who really knows how to write and you will have a top notch sound bite you can use for years!

Don't miss this opportunity to power-ize your invitations. Subliminally, you're setting the tone for the event. People will begin to like you before they ever set foot into your seminar simply by virtue of seeing that others have liked you in the past. Getting endorsements and favorable comments about your seminar is easy and it pays big dividends.

If you question the validity of this strategy, just take a look at the movie pages in your local paper. You will see many movies with "blockbuster" comments, but a closer examination of the fine print will reveal a clever Hollywood trick. Many of these movies quote reviews that appeared in tiny local papers like the Annapolis Public Enterprise or The Hollywood Sound Bite. Many studios will even pay a second-tier reviewer for commentary. Think I'm kidding? Grow up!

Now you can't get Jeffrey Lyons to review your seminar, but any comments that might get someone to think, *"Hey this person seemed to have a great time...maybe I would too,"* are all you need to get the crowd started toward liking you.

People like you when they feel...
Welcome & comfortable

There are several of these "comfort" items on my list and some will sound crazy to you. That's fine. Just ask yourself how you would feel if someone did these things for you. I think you'll see the benefits.

"Is that a space over there?"

Before the seminar even starts...what is one thing that each person in the audience will have to do? **Park the car!**

So here come Ma & Pa Kettle in their late model Oldsmobile driving into the parking lot of the seminar facility. Sure enough, if you've picked a location like a hotel or a restaurant, the place is busy and there's no parking anywhere near the front door. Maybe it's hot outside or worse...it's freezing cold, raining or sleeting! They parked 200 yards away and can barely see the main entrance. They slip on the ice. They curse and swear. They're getting wet or starting to sweat. Slowly, mild negative emotions begin to build.

Who needs that? Why not reserve parking? Talk to the management of the facility. Very often, they will be glad to accommodate you. Cordon off a block of spaces as close as practical to the door and then add the magic touch — **hire a parking attendant** for the evening to direct your people to their reserved space.

"Good evening. Are you here for Mr. Tentpeg's investment seminar? Park right here!"

Wow! Can you imagine the image you've created in the mind of your guests? Your role model for this should be the Disney theme parks. Disney knows that confusion is a negative emotion which impacts the quality of your visit. They take what could be the worst part of your visit — parking a million miles from the front door with a hundred thousand other cars — and they make it FUN! Now you probably can't have a tram carry your people in from Goofy Blue, but the emotional message of reserved parking is big and powerful.

If you wish, you may even want to comment about the parking at some point in your presentation. I might say something like...

"Did everyone find our special parking area OK? We were going to name our parking lot Goofy Green like they do at Disney Land, but considering our topic tonight we thought instead we'd call it Greenspan Blue!"

If you're going to go through the trouble and expense of creating this image by reserving spaces and hiring a valet, you might as well shine a small spotlight on it.

"Hmmm...where's the seminar?"

For the sake of our discussion, let's say that you have chosen to hold your seminar in a typical hotel. Ma & Pa Kettle have made it into the lobby and now they're looking for your seminar. But there's no sign. Or if there is a sign, it's in six point type or on one of those absurd video monitors. So they creep awkwardly up to the registration desk and try to get someone's attention so they can ask *"Where's the investment seminar?"* knowing all the time that they're going to be made to feel stupid and uncomfortable by some clerk who is obviously busy and annoyed.

Again, negative feelings before the event begins. Not good!

Have big signs and lots of them. Twice as many as you think necessary. Signs everywhere with arrows. Signs in the parking lot and at all possible entrances to the facility. People don't always come in the front door.

A sign is much more than something that directs people to the room. It's a symbol of organization and professionalism. It's an emotional buoy that says *"Thanks for coming and we welcome you with open arms!"* which starts the event off with the proper message.

A strategically placed sign also is free advertising to non-attendees wandering around the hotel lobby. Many times, I've had walk-ins come to my seminar just from the sign they saw in the lobby and you never know who you will bump into in a hotel lobby. Quite often, you will find business travelers who have little to do but head up to the room and watch HBO. If your topic is compelling and your sign says, **"Open to the Public"** *and* **"Refreshments Served"**, *you may snare a few big fish.*

Avoid the last minute, magic marker on the yellow pad type sign. But you say, I won't know which way to point the arrows until I get there. Well then, make ten signs each with right, left, and up arrows to cover the contingencies. Then frame them with those overhead projector cardboard frames for a nice touch. Hey...you're selling yourself with every tiny detail here, so spare no effort!

By the way, be sure to collect all your signs before you leave. You don't want to annoy the facility staff by leaving a bunch of signs hanging around. Show everyone that you are a professional, including the facility management.

Festive bunting

Think about it...you've never been to a special event of any kind that didn't have some type of decoration. As a bare minimum, you need a nice big banner with the name of your firm for a backdrop along with an American flag in a stand. The subliminal message is self-evident.

The facility should provide table-coverings and the flag. They will often have the white linen with the side drape for the tables. Be sure they drape only three sides of the table leaving open the area where your legs go. Next to Indian Ocean barnacles, few things in life are more persistent than white linen lint on your clothes from a mis-draped table skirt.

It's OK to have some fun with decorations. Anything you can do within reason and budget to create the feeling in their minds that they are coming to a special, exciting and enjoyable event is great. I've used balloons, pennants, set-up displays, table tent cards, streamers, and enlarged photographs on the walls. You've never been to a special event of any kind where there weren't some decorations or bunting...so try it.

Lighting

Lighting should be bright and comfortable – bright enough for people to see your visuals and take notes at the same time, but not so harsh as to cause glare. Test it out. Sit at a table and try to read the flip chart or the screen at the front of the room. Then try to write a note. If your audience cannot see both you AND their own notes, they will get annoyed.

Avoid dark rooms. If the room is too dark, the audience will either get a headache or fall asleep. Darkness saps energy. You're not likely to get much audience interaction in a dark room. It's hard for you to make eye-contact or read their faces. You might miss valuable audience cues this way...so pour on the lumens.

Do not backlight yourself. Avoid standing in front of windows or reflective surfaces. I attended a presentation at a beautiful country club on a Saturday morning. The room had a great view of the golf course and the speaker thought it would provide a nice back drop to his presentation. Instead, we couldn't see him at all. The brightness of the view drowned him out and all we saw was a dark shadow where his face should have been.

If you insist on a bright background, or have no choice, be sure to light yourself from the front with a hooded flood or a spot light.

Another bad lighting technique is often seen where a speaker stands behind a lectern with her face lit only by the note light on the stand. This is far from the ideal presentation format, yet it's extremely common in those massive slide show presentations we've all attended. If you find yourself in this situation, insist on a spotlight or overhead key light that will make you completely visible without interfering with your projection screen.

Avoid rooms with **only** fluorescent lighting. These throw off a cold, hard color that makes you look pale. Often a facility will supplement the ceiling fluorescence with incandescent sconces, chandeliers or rim lighting. Get to the sight early and mix the lights so that you have a proper balance of visibility and drama.

In an ideal world, lighting would add a sense of drama to the presentation. If you ever find yourself in a position to deliver a presentation from a stage or custom-lighted facility, you can really have a ball. Lighting makes the show. The proper design and use of lighting can enhance every aspect of your presentation.

If you start doing really big seminars, (over 500 people) or doing televised presentations, it will be worthwhile to hire a lighting director to set the lights for the event. Big rooms tend to swallow light and television requires lights that are a different color temperature than stage lights. It's a whole science...believe me. But we'll leave this for the post-graduate class.

Music

It is a well known fact that background music has a subliminal effect on people that can put them in a more responsive and happier frame of mind. Retail stores have found it even gets people to buy more, and at least, it adds to a festive atmosphere for the event.

You might use non-vocal selections from the classical or light jazz category. On occasion, I'll use some vintage Sinatra or big band swing, that seems to always provoke a positive mood. During one stretch of seminars, I actually took selections from Broadway shows that all had money in the theme. This was a lot of fun and set a great tone. It showed effort on my part and drew several comments from the crowd. Hey, it was unique and they loved it.

Whatever music you select should be played at very low volume — just enough to be heard but not too loud as to interfere with conversations. Naturally, you do not want any music playing during your talk, unless you're doing a multi-media presentation where music is integrated into the presentation itself.

Aroma

There is evidence to support the claim that aroma can play a big part in creating a frame of mind in your audience. Just as you might use an air freshener in your home, you could lace the air with pine, vanilla or citrus. A recent study from the University of Michigan reported that a large percentage of men respond to the aroma of cinnamon rolls in a very positive way. It was probably commissioned by Pillsbury.

I used to fly from Los Angeles to New York on the now defunct MGM Airlines. This was the most opulent and comfortable travel experience you could imagine with only 35 seats on the entire plane! The highlight of the trip was the fresh baked chocolate chip cookies. When they brought these out you could see everyone come alive. You would think no one had ever seen a cookie before. There was something about the smell that put us all in a great mood.

So, being ever the student of human nature, I tried this at several seminars. Somewhere near the tail end of the Question & Answer session, before my conclusion, my assistant would bring in some fresh cookies. What a powerful impact! It also was a great way to say *"Thanks for coming,"* and seemed to spark very strong positive emotions in the crowd.

If this aroma thing is too much for you just be sure the room doesn't smell BAD. The North American Limberger Cheese Graters Association or the Cigar Aficionados Club may have just finished using the room before you got there. It's a handicap you don't need.

Sight, smell and sound all add to the feeling of well-being and fun that you want to create during the seminar. None is so critical that you can't survive without it, but with a little effort, you can reap major subconscious rewards by making an audience feel *really* good.

Happy people need
Happy food

Food and refreshments are an interesting subject that cause a lot of concern for some reason. There's no need for too much thought here. Let me suggest two guidelines:

Rule 1: *You are an important financial professional whose clients merit first class treatment. This is your private party and these are your guests — go first class all the way because they deserve nothing less.*

Rule 2: *You're running a business here. You are a skilled professional who has come to educate and enlighten — you don't have to feed the world or go hog wild. The evening is about YOU not the lobster tails.*

Somewhere within those two boundaries is the perfect place to be. In general, you should try to avoid alcohol and overly noisy or messy food like tacos or ribs. Beyond these simple guidelines, the refreshments you serve will depend on your budget.

The facility may be willing to work with you to control refreshment costs. If you plan a series of seminars, let them know you'll be back every month. They may cut you a break on the grub. I will tell you — there is nothing worse than a skimpy or cheap looking spread. Food is an emotional subject all its own. Give your "guests" something to feel good about. It's well worth spending a few extra bucks to make people feel happy and special. And think of the leftovers you'll have...yummm!

I went to a breakfast seminar once where the host was so cheap that they served donuts CUT IN HALF! Imagine this. A *half* a donut! What kind of message do you think he sent his audience. *"Sorry, you're not good enough for a whole donut...you only get half."* What's next? Cut them in steenths and serve them with **toothpicks?**

Play the role of...
The Genial Host

Some would say you get people to like you by first liking them. Before the seminar even begins, people are milling around looking you over. They can probably guess that you're the speaker because you seem to know many people, you're shaking hands and you're the only one wearing a suit...subtle clues like that.

Let them see you with a smile. You are genuinely happy that they came. Frankly, for many of you it's a downright miracle, so let that joy show through. Appear friendly, warm, cordial within the context of professional decorum. Take care not to overdo this, however. If you appear too happy or too friendly you may come off as "slick" like a used-car salesman. You're not here to be "one of the guys," but rather remain in control as the professional who is the center of attention.

Stuck in the mud

Don't get bogged down with friends or existing clients. I've seen it happen a hundred times. Mildred Gotbucks walks in, whips out her latest account statement and monopolizes your time with the eternal saga of her lost dividend. You are not there to handle specific client problems or be buttonholed into private conversations. With a gentle reminder, most people will realize this and gladly wait until the "post-seminar social," to handle specific questions. But if not, this is where a good assistant can really help.

Have the assistant by your side during this greeting period. If any problems arise, you can hand-off to her. What do you think politicians, military leaders and CEOs do? They never go unaccompanied into a "greeting zone." Someone is always attached to them whispering names and deflecting potentially embarrassing situations. Besides, it looks impressive to have an aide de camp at parade rest.

You shouldn't try to meet and greet everyone before the event. This could drain you of crucial energy. I try to simply be visible, look important but friendly. The fewer distractions before you go on the better. If you find yourself cornered by an overly talkative guest before the seminar, arrange a code that will alert your assistant to come over and bail you out.

The pre-game show
They're Watching You

Rule #1 is to arrive well before any guests might show up. That means at least one hour before the scheduled start of the event. Not only will this enable you and your staff to solve any last minute problems, but it will avoid the problem created when Ma & Pa Kettle show up early and you're not there. I promise you this happens all the time. Someone always wants to be the first. They walk in and you're not there...the room's not set up...there's no coffee. What's going through their minds? *"Hey what fools we are. We care more about this seminar than he does."* Not good.

The audience is watching you and forming opinions of you from the first second they arrive. You need to be aware of this and exhibit a calm, cool command of the event. Start by controlling your own emotions. If some unforeseen problem arises — your Sales Assistant's car broke down leaving you to sign people in, the hotel air-conditioner went belly-up two hours ago and your room is a sauna, whatever — you need to handle it calmly and professionally.

I once saw a horrible scene that drove this point home to me more forcefully than anything I can recall. Here was this broker...some Senior V.P. for a major wirehouse. He was obviously angry about something the hotel had not done in preparation for the seminar. I don't know what the specific problem was but this guy was fuming!

He was stomping around the room like a six-year-old in mid tantrum when someone from the hotel came up to see what the problem was. This broker began to berate and chew into this hotel employee IN FULL VIEW of the arriving audience. He was totally unaware of the crowd that had come to complete silence while watching this embarrassing scene. It was so bad, that one couple sitting next to me got up and WALKED OUT in disgust before the seminar even started! This broker will forever wonder why no one took his follow-up phone calls.

As people arrive I want to exude "quiet command" of the situation. No last minute running around shouting and cavorting in confusion. It helps to have a top assistant to handle last-minute details. It helps more to have all the details taken care of long before anyone arrives.

Always...no matter what
Use tables!

There are two main types of seating you will typically run across doing public seminars: **theater-style** where they set up only chairs in rows with an aisle down the middle, or **classroom style** with chairs and tables. Operating under the theory that people will like me better if they feel comfortable, I always use classroom style seating or some other variation with tables like half-round or conference-style. Tables are the key.

If this is your seminar...no matter what...don't ever do a seminar without tables!

Can I put that any more emphatically?

There are a hundred reasons for this but the simplest is that people are ten times more comfortable with tables. They like to have something in front of them on which to rest their arms, their coffee cup or notepad. Tables give them a wider variety of seating positions from which to choose. This becomes critical if you plan to speak for over 30-40 minutes.

Imagine you've got a one-hour presentation. Maybe you've sprung for a few donuts and coffee. And now, you're going to ask people to sit for an hour in a straight-backed chairs with a bear claw in their lap, tightly squeezed into a row with strangers, balancing their coffee and your multi-page hand-out. Trust me, this doesn't go very far toward making them like you.

Also, on a subconscious level, people feel less threatened if they have a table acting as a buffer in front of them. They're much more likely to relax and open up.

Tables also add an element of professionalism to the event. You can pre-arrange customized note paper with the name of the seminar, your name and address on it (see Appendix). You can provide water and those little hard candies. These are small touches that may cost you a few bucks, but they add up to send a subliminal message of power and success.

Tables also allow for dramatic physical flourishes like the **"Table Slammer."** This is where you literally pound the table to punctuate a critical point. You will notice that politicians are doing this more often. They think it demonstrates conviction and seriousness. The problem is that they're usually standing behind a lectern so the result is more of a microphone amplified thump rather than a good, old fashioned slam!

Props

Tables allow you to make use of "props" to illustrate a point. Props are things like coffee cups, pens, paper, whatever is lying on the table. They can be any object that is visible to the audience.

You can come up with dozens of clever uses for props to illustrate all kinds of investment concepts like diversification, risk, and correlation. They provide good visual humor and nearly always lighten things up a bit. It's a great way to make emotional contact with the crowd.

For seminars where you are merely a guest speaker, you may have no choice as to the seating arrangements. I would still try to tell the program people that I wanted tables. If your own seminars are so large that your room can't fit tables...find a different location or split the event into two parts; it's that important.

When they're coming to see you...
Treat them like gold

Getting people to like you may be more difficult for some of you than for others. But every little touch of professionalism, charm and class that makes life easier and more pleasant for your guests will go a long way toward helping this process.

Find your own style and treat these people like gold. They have come to hear you speak and in doing so have bestowed a singular honor upon you. Honor them in return with everything you and your team can do, within reason and budget, to make this the best event they've ever attended.

Wait...what about
HUMOR?

You're probably wondering,

"How can you get people to like you unless you use some humor in your presentation? Why aren't you talking about humor? AAGGHH!!"

Take it easy...you're right. Humor is absolutely vital to the LIKE process. We're going to cover it in detail in Chapter 8, so keep your shirt on!

Director's Notes:

A good table slammer is a punching motion executed by striking the tabletop with the front of the knuckles. Never use the side of the hand. The knuckles make a sharper, crisper sound. If it's done well, it will hurt, but it's worth the effort. Take care to avoid inflicting collateral damage. Watch out for pens, plates, coffee cups and jelly donuts.

CHAPTER 5

UNDERSTANDING

"We are an intelligent species and the use of our intelligence quite properly gives us pleasure. In this respect the brain is like a muscle. When it is in use we feel very good. Understanding is joyous."

Carl Sagan

UNDERSTANDING IS AS EMOTIONAL as love, hate or fear. When you see the look on someone's face as they come up after the seminar and say *"I understand!"* you'll know just how emotional a process it is.

People are scared to death about money. They are bombarded with conflicting and confusing information every day by the media and other investment advisors and they don't know what or whom to trust. But because they fear being taken advantage of, they will often pretend they understand and this pretension hurts them in a very real, financial way.

When I do a seminar, I truly see it as my sacred mission to help them understand and take control of their money. I know that many financial professionals will warn, *"Don't educate them too much or they won't come to you for help."* Quite the contrary. The smarter they are about money and investing, the more they will realize they need your professional guidance. Ultimately, the smarter the investor, (in real terms – not Money Magazine smart), the much more likely it is that our relationship can develop toward a higher level of trust. That's an ideal goal for any financial advisor.

Seminar Format:
An hourglass

Understanding starts with the construction of your presentation. You need to have a clearly-defined structure into which you place all your ideas, support material, motivational themes and action steps. Too many seminars simply flow out of the speaker's mouth with no organization. These "stream-of-consciousness" talks are not likely to produce results for you or for the audience. In fact, they can be counter-productive to creating an image of an organized, clear-thinking professional.

The basic structure you can use for most presentations is like an hourglass. You begin with broad concepts, work down to detailed sub-concepts, facts and support items...then finish with a big picture and a review of the broad concepts. Even in the middle, when you're discussing topics in great detail, you can come back frequently to the broad theme, always relating the details to the big picture.

There are many variations on seminar format and you have to find what works best for you, but a simple bullet-point structure centered around a main theme often works best. For example, here's a very brief outline for a possible seminar on global investing. None of this is cast in stone. It all comes down to tailoring the presentation to your strengths and the audience's interests. The basic hourglass structure is intact.

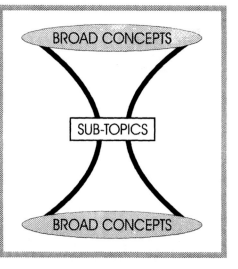

Global Investing in the New World Economy

- Attention grabber opening
- Introduction: Why are we here today?

–Broad overview of the current economic and investment climate.

–Define the problem as a combination of concerns about domestic markets, fear of missed opportunity overseas and the need to properly structure long term investment portfolios.

–What are we going to talk about today?

- Sub Topic #1: Why invest globally?

  How will this strategy improve your performance and reduce your risk?
  1. Greater selection
  2. Faster growth
  3. Better income
  4. Diversification reduces risk
  5. Movement of capital flows

- Sub Topic #2: How to invest globally

  A discussion of the benefits and risks of various investment formats.
  1. Individual securities
  2. ADRs
  3. U.S. companies with foreign exposure
  4. Unit Trusts
  5. Closed-end Funds
  6. Open-end Funds

- Sub Topic #3: Major Global Investment Themes

  The forces and trends at work in the current marketplace and how they're likely to impact your portfolio.
  1. Conservative vs. Aggressive income theme
  2. Conservative growth vs. Aggressive growth theme

- Recap & Summary

  Moving back to and reinforce broad themes

- Questions & Answers

- Conclusion / Call to Action

  End on a positive, optimistic note

This type of format gives you a framework within which to organize your thoughts. The body of the seminar will take on different forms depending on the actual information you are presenting.

However, there are some common characteristics that will enhance the emotional impact of your presentation.

Basic Seminar Design
Logical flow

The overall structure of your presentation should follow a logical path. It should flow easily from one topic to the next with strong connections between each one. Think of your talk as a road trip. On any trip there are waypoints or landmarks that you expect to see. As you approach these, you will know that you're getting closer to your goal. If you stray too far off the main road for too long, you'll get lost. If you digress or get too deep into any sub-theme or topic, the audience may get lost as well. Always bring them back to the main topic — connect your comments to a pattern and refer back to the main theme often.

The goal of the presentation structure and the content should be to break down large, seemingly complex ideas or problems into easy-to-understand and action-oriented solutions. It's a logical process with a well-defined objective.

> *Talk about logical flow — I was doing a global investing seminar for a young broker in New York City. He was new at public seminars but was very eager to try his hand. He came to me a day before the event and said that all he wanted to do was to open the seminar by making some simple welcoming remarks and then to introduce me. I told him that this wouldn't be the ideal seminar structure for his own credibility, but he insisted and I agreed since this seemed to be all that he could handle.*

> *Instead of sticking to the gameplan, he got up, said "Hello & thanks for coming." and dove into a detailed discussion of currency hedging! I was stunned. I thought I was in a time warp. The audience was sitting there in shock wondering if they were in the right room.*

> *It took me a good ten minutes just to repair the confusion and get everyone back onto the main road.*

He must have focused on my credibility comment and became overly anxious to show everyone how much he knew, (a VERY common seminar problem in our industry). So he leaped into a very complex topic with no preparation. Now there's nothing wrong with wanting to look smart, except this over eagerness caused him to short-circuit the logical format of the discussion and thus risk the entire event

The exact same sub-topic or any complex discussion placed later in the seminar would have worked just fine. The audience would have had a chance to mentally warm up and his talk would have been much better received and understood. The way he did it, right at the opening introduction, it was absurd and very damaging. The audience was immediately Lost in Space with Will, Penny and Dr. Smith never to be found again.

Whenever you have a big or complicated subject to discuss, always remember the elephant analogy. The question: *"How do you eat an elephant?"* The answer: *"One bite at a time."* If you break your talk down into small chunks and take it in logical step-by-step precision, even nuclear physics is easy to grasp.

"What this means to you is this..."
Make it real and make them feel

Every speaker has learned the old maxim:
Tell them what you're going to tell them.

Tell them.

Tell them what you told them.

That's a little simplistic, but the basic truth of this advice is sound. For maximum seminar results, add two important sentences to that maxim:
Tell them why it's important to them.

Tell them how they should feel about it.

Everything you say should have some emotional meaning to the audience. Often, the meaning is obvious, but sometimes it's necessary to show them the meaning in very specific terms. For example, we know that diversification is important. We understand the relationship between interest rates and inflation. To us, this stuff is elementary because we live, eat, sleep and breathe it every day. To them it's like brain surgery. Investing scares the Hell out of the public and they will vapor lock easily if you don't make your talk relevant to them on a very basic emotional level.

When the situation calls for it, go ahead and be very direct with them. If you want to be sure that they are going to understand your presentation, you might insert a brief commentary like this:

"Folks...a lot of what we're going to talk about tonight may seem very complicated or difficult to understand. Some of it may even seem rather esoteric or meaningless to you at first. Let me just stop right here for a second because this is critical."

"Everything we are going to discuss here tonight is very important to you in a real way — it all affects your money — and your money affects your life. And none of this...absolutely nothing we will talk about here is beyond your understanding. I will do my very best to be certain that you all are completely comfortable with everything we've got to cover. And if there comes a point in the seminar when you're 'a might bewildered' as Daniel Boone used to say...just stop me...and we'll get you back on board."

"When you leave here tonight, you will all have a better, clearer and more confident grasp of the important trends affecting your financial future. So much so, in fact, that I want each of you to go out and buy one of these flip charts and do this exact seminar at your next dinner party. You can amaze and astound your neighbors! You know...just clear the table...get out your multi-colored magic markers and go!"

This kind of a discussion may seem strange to you, but it falls under the heading of pre-emptive emotional control. You want them to feel something, so tell them very specifically what you want and expect them to feel...and they will feel it.

In this case, you want them to generate the emotion of understanding, so you're going to plant the seed early in the seminar that they WILL understand your talk. Give them a clear visual picture of the way they will feel and act after they leave the event. For this you use the zany (and very physical) image of the dinner party home seminar to cement this feeling of understanding.

It's up to you to...
Find the dragon

Begin the seminar by defining the problem or the "conflict" that brought the people out in the first place. Why are they here? What are they looking for? Are they suffering from low interest rates? Are they missing an exciting growth opportunity? Are they being buried alive in taxes? There had to be some emotional reason they got off their butts and came to see you . . . what was it? First, find it and then, re-define the reason for them **in your own words:**

> *"Do you want to know why you're here tonight? What was it that moved you away from the TV and motivated you to take valuable time to drive here and listen to me? I'll tell you why you're here..."*

Define a broad-based problem that hits a common emotional chord in all of them. This is the great thing about doing your own seminars — you get to define all the problems and the solutions in your own words. What more could anyone want?

> *"Folks, you're here tonight because you can't live on 5% returns! People all across this country are struggling with this same problem. Some of them are retired and living on fixed income, some are still trying to grow a nestegg, some are just starting out, it doesn't matter who you are or how much money you have . . . we are all affected by the same economic environment and the same problems. (PAUSE) Tonight, we're going to find some answers!"*

Try to include every group you see in the audience. You want them all to see the same dragon so they will be simultaneously awed when you slay it right before their eyes. The good news is that you get to pick the dragon!

Unify the emotional state

The other benefit of this re-defining process takes us back to the previous chapter on LIKE. Remember we talked about audience synergy, the group dynamic of shared emotional response. When you successfully define a broad investment problem in emotional terms that everyone can understand and feel you will have psychologically locked the audience together.

This is essential early in the seminar and should be constantly reinforced throughout the event. By bringing them together emotionally, you can use this connection to enhance and strengthen the intensity of their response to you. They will resonate as a nearly unified entity. Once this happens, you can really deliver a powerful message that will motivate nearly all of them to action.

This is one of the critical keys to the high close rates you will experience as a result of your seminars. I'm talking about 75% or 85% closing within 90 days! That's how positive and exciting a tool this can be if you master these techniques.

Throughout history, the most stirring moments in the annals of oral communication have been marked by those speakers who could bring a group together emotionally, and then lead them toward a solution defined by the speaker. From Marc Antony to Ronald Reagan, the best public speakers have understood and used this process. You can too.

Teach them well
And they will love you

Teaching investment concepts can be easy and fun. Even the most complex subject can be broken down into understandable elements. And the process of understanding is fun because it has a direct impact on people's lives. The process of teaching an investment concept to your audience can be exciting...like a mystery novel slowly revealed. Let me give you an example by looking at how I teach one such topic in my seminars. You might like it...you might not. Your style is what's important, so don't think you have to do it my way. You also might disagree with my facts or statistics...that's OK. The process is what's important.

Non-Correlated Diversification
The "visual build" at work

This is told as part of a global investing seminar. It would also work with any discussion of Modern Portfolio Theory. It's a great example of a "visual build." This is a technique of combining your words with a visual aid that you draw slowly, in stages, only revealing parts of the drawing as you teach the concept.

Folks, so far tonight, I've given you a few reasons for considering global investments in your portfolio...but now I want to show you the key to the whole thing. This is the one that gets me the most excited and I want to spend a minute on it because if you understand this...you will be a long way toward understanding how money works and how you can succeed in reaching all your financial goals.

Notice how we hit a few emotions here and how we worked back up to the major benefits of understanding how money works and reaching financial goals. I want them to see this segment as a critical part of the evening and I want to get their juices flowing.

Let's say that you have all your money right now in the U.S. One hundred percent of your portfolio is U.S. based...either stocks or bonds or a combination...it doesn't matter. Let's draw this on the board because it's going to be a lot easier to understand as we get into it.

By the way...the first person who ever drew what I'm about to show you...won the Nobel Prize in Economics...so I'm not making this up. We're going to have a graph with two lines.

Draw the vertical line, write RETURN with the arrow and pause.

The vertical line measures the annual rate of return on your

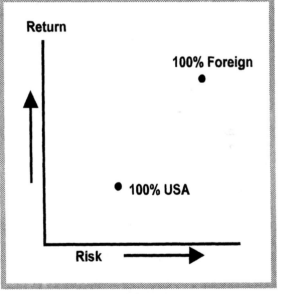

portfolio measured in percentage terms. *The horizontal line measures something that's critical to any portfolio...and that's RISK.*

Now draw the horizontal line, write the word risk with the arrow. You can explain standard deviation if you wish.

Remember we said that your portfolio is 100% in the US. For our example, let's assume you are in an index fund that matches the performance of the S&P 500...OK? Now, for any portfolio, there is a certain historical rate of return and a certain level of risk. So we can actually place a dot at the exact point on this graph that will represent your portfolio because we know these numbers very well.

Draw a dot and write 100% USA.

Remember we said earlier that the foreign markets, over time, have outperformed the US market by a substantial margin. We can also put a dot on the graph to represent the foreign markets because we have all those risk and return numbers as well.

Draw the EAFE dot and write 100% foreign. Explain the EAFE Index and stress that it is a diversified index of several countries, not just a single foreign market. Chances are you will get questions about specific country funds or regions and this concept of a diversified overseas portfolio will become important.

You'll notice that I drew this dot further out along the risk line. Why is that? Well you know that the greater return you want, the greater risk you must be willing to take...right? So if you took 100% of your money and invested it overseas...you would get a better annual return...but you would also be taking a lot more risk. Does this make sense so far? OK...now we get to the interesting part.

There is a line between these two points that actually shows the return and risk for any possible combination of foreign and US portfolios. This line shows what will happen as you begin to add foreign stocks to a US portfolio. The results are very interesting.

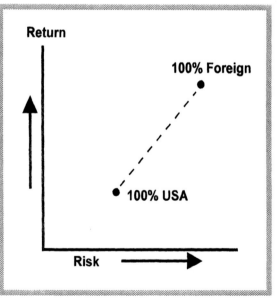

As we move overseas, what do you think happens to the risk and return?

What does the line that connects these two points look like? Doesn't it look like this?

Draw dashed line connecting the two points.

This is common sense right? What happens as you reach for higher and higher return? You take greater and greater risk...right? PAUSE

Well, that's what we've always been taught and that's what common sense tells us but guess what...that's wrong! Here's why this fellow won the Nobel Prize! By the way, his name was Markowitz and he was a mathematician at Bell Labs in New Jersey. So some good things do come out of New Jersey.

The attempt at mild humor breaks the tension I'm obviously trying to create here. Just enough tension to get them excited and ready for the grand finale. Do not take any questions or brook any interruptions at this point. You should complete the thought in one continuous flow if it's to have the impact you desire.

The actual line that connects these two points IS NOT a straight line...instead it curves like this.

Draw the curved, boomerang line.

Folks, this little curve is the key to modern portfolio theory and it is the basis for proper asset allocation. This is critical, so please follow me here.

As we move from a 100% US portfolio slowly adding money to a foreign portfolio our rate of return goes up...

Trace your finger along the curve.

and what happens to our risk...our risk

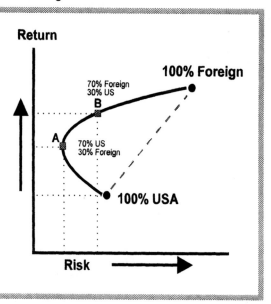

goes down! *Until you reach a point on the curve right here where the risk is lowest (the first square). Right at this point, the mixture in your portfolio is 70% US and 30% foreign! Taking thirty percent of your portfolio and moving it into diversified foreign investments actually gives you the lowest possible risk in a given portfolio.*

Draw vertical line from point A down to the RISK Axis.

But there's another critical point on this curve. maybe you've already noticed it. Start right here at your 100% US portfolio and draw a straight

*line up to this point (second square) and you now have a portfolio that
is giving you the exact same risk as a 100% domestic portfolio...BUT
look what's happened to your annual return!*

Draw a horizontal line from point B to the RETURN axis.

*You have dramatically increased you annual return and taken the exact
same risk you're taking right now in a 100% US portfolio.*

*A lot more return for the same amount of risk...or a little added return
for a lot less risk...it's your choice. But THIS is the beauty of going global
and THIS is why we are here tonight.*

*This phenomenon has a very technical term. We call it non-correlated
diversification. It is the key to good portfolio design and understanding
how it works will make a tremendous difference in your life. It is, in fact,
the basis of all the work we do. And when we do it today, we're
considering not just two asset classes....but fifteen. We take all these
variables and we "optimize" your portfolio by giving you the best rate
of return with the least risk. Not bad huh?*

Don't panic!

Look, I know some of my facts and the shape of my curve might
not be perfectly in line with your numbers. This was simply an
illustration of a value-added teaching point and how you present a
complex concept at a seminar. You can see how easy-to-understand
the presentation was. Everyone in the room will be able to follow this
and they will feel tremendously empowered by the knowledge.

The key is to draw the chart slowly, allowing them time to digest
the spoken words while they see the corresponding picture. In most
seminars, a complex visual like this would be done in one detailed
slide. This forces you to explain your way through a maze of lines
and dots and it makes the whole explanation very confusing to the
audience. By using visual builds, you can take the time needed to
reveal a concept slowly, one element at a time.

This style works with nearly every investment concept you
might want to discuss in a seminar. Many in the audience will feel as
though they understand money for the first time...and they will have
you to thank for that understanding!

Language and understanding
Use jargon carefully

Some people will caution you to *"Avoid jargon!"* But we work
in a jargon-ized profession, it's very difficult to avoid. Jargon sets

you apart as an expert with a unique language. As long as you remember that you're not talking to a room of investment bankers or NYSE specialists, it's OK to drop an occasional industry-specific word or phrase, but you must explain it.

True, today's audiences are much more knowledgeable than those of only a few years ago, but whenever you use an unexplained piece of techno-babble you create a mental fork in the road. Some people will simply lose the path and not catch up for many minutes if at all. Take the time to explain key phrases they NEED to understand to make them better, smarter investors.

Some words that cause confusion include very commons ones like "equities," "the long-bond," "optimize," "NAV," "closed-end," "yield curve," "discount or premium," and my favorite, the ubiquitous "basis point."

*Most "civilians" have no idea what a basis point is. And worse yet, when you say "basis point" they hear the word "points" and their mind immediately races to the only other time in their lives when they heard the word point — which was when? When they bought their home! Now when you're getting a home mortgage are "points" a good thing or a bad thing? Their minds make a primitive, limbic connection, **"Points - Bad!"** Like Frankenstein with **"Fire - Hurt!"** You've lost them for a good five minutes.*

One exception

There is one exception to this rule of explaining jargon — a powerful technique we will discuss in the Chapter on Confidence called the Teaching Take-Away. You should use this when you want to impress them with the depth of your knowledge and send a subliminal message that says, *"Look, I am the expert and you are the public. As smart as you think you are, you can't possibly match my level of understanding."*

Be sure they're still with you
Check the map

If there is one thing that marks a top quality speaker from an ordinary one, it would be what I call the *"audience mind-meld."* You should watch for certain clues that will tell you whether or not they're following you.

Be on guard for any fidgeting, whispering, yawning or looks of bewilderment. The first sign of these should cause you to check their progress or change the pace and delivery of the presentation. Positive signs like head nodding, note-taking, intense eye-contact and timely laughter tell you that you're on the right track.

> *One traditional speaker's trick is to listen for coughing or throat clearing as a sign that the audience is getting bored. This can be misleading, however, depending on the refreshments you've served prior to the seminar. Often, dairy foods like cheese or chocolates will cause excess moisture in the throat and lead to a spate of post snack throat clearing. If you served no refreshments and they're still gagging and sputtering, you might want to pick up the pace a bit.*

In the absence of these obvious clues, it can't hurt to ask *"Is that clear? Is this concept beginning to make sense? Are we together on that?"* Don't do it every other sentence or it will become annoying, but do it at any critical juncture before moving on to the next waypoint. For example, in the middle of a detailed sub-theme of your major thesis, pause, take a breath (literally) and check the map to remind them of where I'm going with this thought.

> **"OK, (PAUSE) we are looking at the relationship between inflation and interest rates. What I've just shown you is the history of inflation during the past sixty five years, so now, let's tie that into to the movement of long-term bond rates. What you're going to see is an incredible connection here. This is one very important reason that we are so bullish on the coming market environment — because low inflation means low interest rates and low rates are great for the stock market. It has been throughout history and it will be again!"**

In this way, we round up all the stragglers and get everyone back onto the broad theme.

Never forget
The ultimate goal

Your ultimate goal in conducting this seminar is NOT to turn the public into investment experts. It's to get them to take some kind of action — in most cases, that means an appointment. But, they're not going to do a damn thing unless they understand you. It's OK if they don't ALWAYS understand everything you say or do. In truth, they're paying you to know this stuff so that they don't have to. But in a public seminar, where they've given their time to come hear your message, they expect you to go out of your way to be understandable.

This is not easy. In fact, many of the top industry gurus who regularly present to the public on behalf of major securities firms or mutual fund houses regularly forget this concept. I saw one well-known and brilliant expert do a public presentation recently, and it was terrible. He stood motionless behind a large lectern in the dark to the side of a huge projection screen. His entire presentation consisted of one slide after another of these complex charts and graphs. If it wasn't for the occasional question from the audience you would have thought you were listening to a tape machine.

I swear to you — not 10% of that audience was any smarter than when they walked in. Judging by the murmurs I heard in the crowd during the event, they were more confused *after* he finished. It would have been a thousand times better if he simply talked to the audience. He had a great message but was so wrapped up in the high-brow intellectualism of his presentation, that he wasted everyone's time.

What about...
Visual aids

There is no doubt that visual aids help people understand a topic better. They nearly double the retention rate of information, as well. The question becomes, which type of visual aid works best and how should you use them?

This is a controversial subject. Personally, I have never been a fan of elaborate visual aids (slides, videos, overheads, etc.). Instead, I like a simple flip chart and a minimalist approach to visuals. With the rapid advances in presentation technology today, you've got some exciting possibilities and I'm reviewing my opinion on this subject.

In the typical investment seminar, you will have one of three visual aid formats to select from: flip charts, overheads and slides. More and more people are turning to computer multi-media presentations and I find myself doing more presentations with PowerPoint and an In-Focus machine. I suspect that this format will make slide projectors obsolete over time, but these are still very expensive systems and represent only a small fraction of what's occurring right now on the public seminar circuit.

Turn to the chapter on **Visual Aid Pros & Cons** for a complete discussion of the major formats you have available today. Whatever visual aid or combination you choose, there are a few things to keep in mind.

1. Don't overload the audience on visuals. Instead, use them sparingly. A good rule of thumb with slides and overheads is to have one visual for every three minutes of presentation and to present one major point per visual. Don't try to crowd the visual with too much data. Not only does this begin to get cluttered, but you can no longer take advantage of the transition phase to set up your next major point.

2. Keep them simple. It's so tempting today to use the four-dimensional floating bar charts and the rotating scattergrams and a host of other information-packed slides. Personally, I'd scrap them all. I prefer big, bold, easy-to-see shapes like circles for pie charts and rectangles and lines. *Hey, Einstein taught General Relativity on a blackboard...you need something more?*

3. Keep your text bullets short. People hate bullet points that are really paragraphs in disguise. Bullet means just that — POW! No more than five words in a sentence fragment is just fine. And don't use 20 bullets on one slide. The size of the typeface must be clearly visible in the back of the room. This usually limits you to six bullet points.

4. Clear the visual before you discuss it. Whenever you pop a visual up on the screen the audience scrambles to understand what they're looking at. This creates a moment when you no longer have control of the audience...the screen does. Instead, tell them exactly what they're seeing.

For bullet points, do the same thing. Quickly read each of the bullets, top to bottom, and then go back up to the first bullet to begin your expanded discussion.

If you don't do this, and instead start talking in detail about the first bullet point, the audience will begin to read down the list and not concentrate on what you're saying. By clearing the visual, you keep them with you and you control the movement of their attention on the slide. And remember, take your time. If a visual is important enough to include in your presentation, it's important enough to handle correctly.

5. Use visual builds whenever possible. A visual build prevents this "read-ahead" problem and is an excellent way to display information. With a build, each bullet point comes up one-at-a-time and when bullet #2 pops up, bullet #1 fades to gray or some other color of lesser visibility. This forces the audience to concentrate on the current bullet and stay with you — all of which increases understanding.

Creating builds with slides is expensive because they require multiple slides for each bullet chart and graph. Overheads are easier because you can place an opaque sheet of paper over the items you want to hide and reveal them one at a time. Flip charts allow for natural builds since you can only write one thing at a time.

This is one of those times when technology is your friend. Computer presentation packages like Microsoft Powerpoint or Freelance Graphics allow builds and various "reveals" in their slide show presentations. Get yourself a good laptop computer, some software and an In-Focus machine and you could really have some fun doing slide-type presentations!

6. Master the transitions. A transition is the presentation segment between two visuals. It's what you say after you're done with the points on the current visual in preparation for the next visual. It could be as short as a few seconds when you're using the slide projector, or much longer when you're creating the visuals with a flip chart. When it comes to slides and overheads, the transition is as important if not MORE important than the slide itself.

The transitions prepare the audience to receive visual information and are very valuable as a way to increase your credibility with the audience. For those of you who are using slides and sticking to the script exclusively, the transition may be the only time when you are speaking your own words rather than merely regurgitating what marketing prepared for you. You should give much thought to the design of intelligent transition commentary and focus on the delivery using all the emotional techniques you're reading about in this book.

You can no doubt tell that I strongly recommend you avoid being a "parrot", but I also know that's where most financial professionals get their start in this world of public presentations. The sooner you can develop your own content and supplement what marketing gives you with your own words...the better you're going to do with seminars. For now, the transitions may be your only outlet, so use them well.

7. Check your visuals from all points in the room. Be sure that they can be seen from the back and the sides. Sit down in a chair when you're testing, because the audience will be seated as well. They cannot understand what they cannot see.

8. Proofread everything. Be absolutely certain you have carefully reviewed all your visual material. Nothing detracts from a professional presentation more than a misspelled word. Don't assume that someone in headquarters has done this. Spelling and grammar are rare skills in today's work place and quality control is often spotty.

9. Make visuals attractive. But don't go crazy. Use colors that compliment and support your theme. People trust blue. Green calms them. They fear red and orange. Use yellow and black for bold statements. Pictures and patterns for slides and overheads are fun, but should not clutter the story.

Visual aids will indeed help the process of understanding, but they must take second place to a well-designed presentation with an intelligent and logical structure. Don't let them rule you, they are mere servants.

There is another group of tools which you can use to significantly increase understanding and have a lot of fun in the process.

Pass it around
Physical aids

These are "physical" because they are three-dimensional, real things that you have on hand as illustrative teaching tools. One of the best set of these PAs is used regularly by representatives of a major mutual fund company. I've been to a dozen of their presentations and I'm amazed each time by the fun the audience has with this segment of the program. It's very exciting to watch.

For a discussion of inflation, for example, the speaker pulls out a dollar bill. Then he asks the audience to give him a reasonable inflation rate expectation for the next twenty years. The number ends up to four percent. He then unfolds another dollar bill that's attached to the first one — except this one is four percent small than the original dollar.

"Now that doesn't look too bad.", he says, "But here's another four percent...and another four percent and another and another..."

Each time he unfolds another, slightly smaller bill until he gets down to twenty years worth of inflation and a tiny little dollar.

This is a blast! It's so simple and yet so effective in front of a room. Immediately, they understand the effect inflation has on their money.

Turn the stack around and you've got a great way to show people how much income they're going to need in twenty years.

Another, even more dramatic example is the way he shows an audience the relative returns from inflation, T-bonds, blue-chip stocks and small-cap growth stocks. For each asset class he pulls out a stack of bills.

"What would your dollar have grown to if you had invested in Treasury bonds sixty five years ago? Anyone have an idea? Well...here it is. Your dollar would be worth eighteen dollars today."

He pulls out a wrapped stack of 18 dollar bills.

"What about in blue-chip stocks, like the S&P 500? Well, one dollar would be worth $690!"

He starts to pull out stack after stack of dollar bills piling them up right next to the puny stack of 18 dollars. There is a lot of room for improvisation during this process and you can have a ball with the audience while you're doing this.

"Well if those are blue chips, what about small-cap growth companies. I'll see your $690 and I'll raise you one...two...three thousand dollars."

Now, he's got a monster stack of bills...and the audience's complete attention. These are marvelous ways to drive home certain points in your seminar.

Physical aids can also include stock certificates, newspaper articles, foreign currency or actual products made by the companies you may be discussing in your presentation. Nick Murray, the best-selling author of several investment marketing books and noted industry speaker, uses a business card laminated with two postage stamps on the back — an 8-cent stamp from 1970 and today's 32-cent stamp to illustrate inflation's effect on everyday life. Brilliant!

Once, while doing a series of global seminars, I went out and bought several dozen common items made by foreign companies that the typical person would be very likely to find around the house. I arranged these on a table in the front of the room and referred to them throughout the event. Afterwards, I gave them out as fun little prizes.

The whole thing cost $50 for each seminar and really helped the audience understand how deeply they were already involved with foreign companies — they were using their products every day.

Reinforce your message with
Handouts

Handouts are great for two reasons: they can be used during the seminar to keep the audience mentally active and involved with your talk and they act as memory aids after the seminar or a segment of the seminar is completed.

The Master of the Handout has to be Joel Weldon, a well-known superstar on the corporate seminar circuit. Joel uses his customized handouts as notes relieving you of the need to write during his presentation. (In fact, you could never keep up with his pace if you *were* taking notes.) He controls the distribution of these handouts very carefully because he doesn't want you to read ahead of him, so he gives them out after he completes a discussion segment and then quickly reviews the handout noting key points. This works great and it allows you to stay focused on him.

Generally, it's better to distribute your handouts AFTER the seminar, with the exception of those note-type handouts mentioned above and customized note paper. Your handouts may include:

- **Prospectuses for any of the investment ideas you might be discussing**
- **Your own newsletter**

- Company research reports
- Copies of pertinent articles
- A bio sheet on you
- A bibliography of reading material on your topic

For special audiences where you really want to generate involvement and deep understanding, use a **storyboard workbook.** (See Appendix)

In this book, you've got miniature pictures of the actual slides you're using with space at the right of each slide for them to take notes. The storyboard workbook allows the audience to follow your presentation in detail from point to point.

The benefit of this kind of approach is grounded in psychological research that says, when you really want someone to learn something, get them to write it down. The process of transferring knowledge from right to left brain increases retention by upwards of 90%.

Admittedly, this is not for every seminar, but if you're making a detailed presentation to a board of directors pitching for a $50 million pension plan, and you know you're only going to get one shot at helping them understand your message — this level of sophistication may be warranted and very valuable.

For advanced speakers
Audio & video tapes

Why not offer an audio tape of your presentation to attendees. This is a great way to reinforce your message long after they've gone home...and it can be a super source of referral business. This is standard practice at all the major conventions and trade shows.

Video is more difficult and expensive, because you're going to need a camera-person if you're doing the seminar correctly — that is to say moving around and engaging the audience. But for those of you at the top of your craft, I strongly recommend this as a powerful differentiation tool.

Subliminal benefits of taping

When you attend a seminar and notice that the speaker is being video or audio-taped — what do you think? Many people assume that the speaker is important, or at least the presentation is somehow going to be worth recording.

Simply by wearing a lapel mike or having a tape recorder in the room, you have elevated the perception of quality and respect in the minds of the audience. The implication that your words might have impact beyond that room lends an air of power to your presentation.

The final benefit to taping yourself is for training purposes. Every great athlete and performer watches or listens to themselves on tape. You are no different. If you feel the need to improve your skills, you should be taping everything, including phone conversations. Self-improvement begins with self-understanding.

CHAPTER 6

RESPECT

"I can't get no respect."
Rodney Dangerfield

R ESPECT IS A MAJOR EMOTIONAL goal of every seminar. You want to convey an image of importance, power and knowledge. You want the audience to respect your abilities and professional judgment. You want them to feel fortunate and special to be at your seminar and ultimately to be your client.

This may sound pompous, overblown and way too ego-inflating, but all of it can be accomplished in very subtle and pleasant ways without the negative connotations you might assume.

The good news is that the audience WANTS to respect you. So you're already halfway there.

In nearly all cases, the amount of respect you generate in any given audience is directly proportional to the quality and emotional impact of your presentation. In short, the better your seminar, the more they will respect you as an investment professional. And the more they respect you, the better your seminar can be. It sounds circular and it is, but it's also very real.

This doesn't always hold true for other financial professionals. Mutual fund portfolio managers, for example, are often judged on an inverse scale of presentation ability. The better they are as presenters, often the worse they are perceived as money managers. One financial advisor friend has what he calls the "Nerd Factor." A portfolio manager who can really motivate and excite an audience would scare him into liquidating the fund.

Why respect?

Part of my thinking for this approach is admittedly philosophical. I don't believe that a meaningful business relationship can ever develop unless the clients respect you and your professional abilities. But in today's competitive world, we face tremendous forces that tear away at the respect for our profession. The media consistently feeds the do-it-yourself mentality and erodes trust in professional advice. The net result is that many investors who need your help do not seek it or accept it when it's offered. You may even find that your advice and recommendations are being questioned more frequently by many of your top clients.

Thus, in a seminar environment, and in business itself on a broader scale, you cannot expect to command respect by your mere presence. Instead, your actions, words, delivery and emotional effectiveness must earn respect over time.

The good news is that there are several specific techniques that will build a climate of respect and significantly increase the likelihood of turning your audience into life-long clients.

Respect starts with . . .
The Introduction

An introduction seems too basic a concept to warrant much discussion but, in fact, it's an important theatrical device for setting the tone of respect for the entire seminar. No speaker of substance or authority would ever jump up to the lectern without a proper introduction, so don't you do it either.

The introduction has a physical benefit as well as a psychological one. It acts as a buffer during the noisy transition phase at the beginning of the meeting. People may be concluding their conversations, getting a last cup of coffee or just finding their way to their seats. You, as the "star of the show," should not try to talk over that activity. In musical theater it's called the overture — something to let everyone settle into the proper mood for the spectacle to follow. You're the spectacle here, so be introduced.

The introduction may also be the place to make any administrative announcements *(i.e., parking validations, bathroom locations, use of recording devices, etc.).*

Who does it and what do they say?

Ideally, the introducer would be someone of prestige like your Branch Manager, a fellow advisor or someone known to the group. In a pinch, it can be anyone with some "stage presence" and an audible voice. You may have a very capable assistant who would be great or you might consider partnering up with a colleague to handle introductions at each other's seminars. In either case, practice the introduction just as you would any other part of the seminar...it's that important.

The introduction should be smooth and energetic. It takes less than one minute but it should build a sense of anticipation and excitement in the audience. Something like this:

> *"Ladies & Gentlemen, thank you all for coming tonight. (PAUSE) This is a very exciting and confusing time in the world of investing. Today, many people are facing some of the most important financial decisions of their lives — and they're asking questions. (PAUSE) Tonight, we'll try to give you some answers and clear up some of the confusion."*

> *(Transition, smile, deliver casually but with enthusiasm)*

> *"You are in for a very EXCITING and ENJOYABLE evening."* (speak slowly)

> *"Our guest speaker is (title) with XYZ Incorporated. He brings with him some very impressive credentials and experience."* (Two or three bullets on who you are and your more important credentials.)

Don't worry — as sparse as your credentials may be, you can find one or two worthwhile items of experience to mention VERY briefly. Or, go with #2 below.

> *"He brings with him a unique and dynamic perspective* to our profession and we're very excited to have him here tonight!"*

*This can be safely said about anyone.

"Please welcome (pause) Joe Tentpeg!" or

"It's my pleasure to introduce (pause) Mr. Joe Tentpeg!"

Now that's nice! You've set the audience up for your entrance with the appropriate amount of enthusiasm and prepared them for a very enjoyable session. Have you gone overboard? I don't think so. None of what we said was too obnoxious or distasteful.

Always end on your name

Notice how the introduction itself ends on your name. This is a hundred times more dramatic than what most people do which is leak the name early in the introduction. You want your name to ring in their ears while you move to your place. It creates a much more powerful feeling of respect.

The introduction must be memorized

At your own seminar, the introduction should be completely memorized. It's less effective if the introducer has to read your credentials from a note card, especially if they're supposed to know you. They should also avoid tired phrases like *"let me turn the meeting over to..."* In Toast Masters, we had to pay a $5.00 fine if we ever said those words.

Use an introduction card for groups

If you' re the guest speaker at a club or banquet, the introducer may not know you. This gives you little control over the quality of the introduction. I've spoken to groups where the person doing the introduction was fantastic. They set me up so professionally that I could have been speaking ancient Greek and the crowd would have loved it. Most of the time, it's not that good, and very often, it's abysmal!

Whenever you're a guest at a club or organization, find out who will be doing your introduction as quickly as you can. Give that person a 3x5 card with bullet points of your desired introduction printed in easy-to-read text. It will be greatly appreciated, I assure you. And you might want to bring two or three introduction cards with you. Often, the introducer may switch at the last minute and you don't want to search through the crowd looking for the person to whom you gave your introduction card.

Here's a sample introduction card.

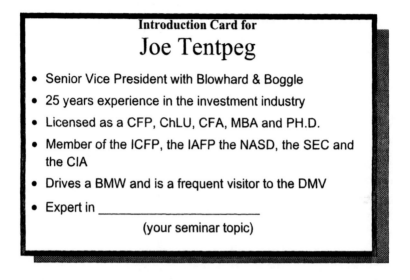

Introduction Card for
Joe Tentpeg

- Senior Vice President with Blowhard & Boggle
- 25 years experience in the investment industry
- Licensed as a CFP, ChLU, CFA, MBA and PH.D.
- Member of the ICFP, the IAFP the NASD, the SEC and the CIA
- Drives a BMW and is a frequent visitor to the DMV
- Expert in _____

(your seminar topic)

Before we move on, you might be wondering about that last bullet, so let me pound the table for a second.

Don't ever hesitate to say that you are an expert. To the public, and particularly to your audience, you damn well better be a specialist in the topic or you shouldn't be there speaking in the first place. And to carry that a step further — what the heck are you doing in the investment business at all if you're not an expert?

I know it's popular to downplay your knowledge, but that's the first thing you've got to stop if you plan to be successful with seminars. I'm absolutely NOT saying that you should exaggerate, boast or overdo any of this. You don't need to. Compared with 99.99% of the U.S. population, you ARE an expert in this field, so be proud and use it to your advantage. No matter how casual, comfortable and down to Earth this audience may appear, they want to hear expertise, not rambling opinions from a "civilian" no smarter than themselves.

Bond to the audience

If you're doing a seminar for a club or other organization you might insert a line into the introduction that will help bond you to the group or lead you into an opening. A few years ago, at a local sportsmans' club, I added the line —**Amateur trapshooter.**

This was a true statement that allowed me to open in a much more relaxed mode and yet still gain respect in a subtle way by saying,

"If I did as poorly in the market as I do at the trap range, I would NEED that shotgun (PAUSE) to hunt for FOOD!"

High & Mighty Exhaulted Grand Poobah
Use a title

If you have a title, now is the time to use it. Titles sound impressive and may also highlight your qualifications. The introducer should speak your title slowly and with appropriate awe. Don't skimp on the verbal emphasis here. Words like *"Senior Vice President," "Member of the prestigious Chairman's Circle"* and all the other grand attachments that accompany your name must be enunciated with energy.

Perhaps you're the Retirement Plans Coordinator or a club-level producer, whatever. Use them...they work. You should orchestrate the mixture of titles in your introduction to end on the most impressive sounding one. Play with this and have some fun.

If you don't have a title, get one. Become a product coordinator or office specialist or something. Get your CFP or CFA or CLU or whatever you can that adds professional value to your career. Not only will you have something powerful to say in your introduction, but more importantly, you'll benefit from the knowledge gained.

By the way, most of the audience doesn't know (and doesn't need to know) that titles at many investment firms are often based on gross commissions. After all, "Vice President" means you're next in line to the President...right?

I'm half kidding here, but let me tell you a true story of how a title can carry weight.

> *When I was buying my first house, I was considering which real estate agent to use and I picked one agent because she was a* **"Member of The Million Dollar Roundtable."** *To me, that sounded very impressive, and she did a great job. When I thought about it a little deeper it dawned on me that a realtor who sold $1,000,000 worth of property earned 6% commission. But that was split between the buying*

and selling realtor. That was further split between the realtor herself and the broker. She netted roughly $15,000 in annual commissions — pre-tax. Hardly the kind of superstar I was led to assume from the title, but the title did its job like a charm. It allowed that agent to plant an image of tremendous success in my mind.

The introduction fulfills their expectation

I know that I'm beating this introduction stuff into the ground, but remember, the seminar is an emotional process. Every audience has certain expectations when they attend an event. From experience, they know that the more important the speaker, the more polished the introduction. They expect this. Do less and you're cheating them of this emotional fulfillment and diminishes your stature, not disastrously, but a little bit. I'm not suggesting you play "Hail to the Chief," but I can't over-emphasize the power of subtle and subliminal processes like this.

Finally, remember that the introducer's job is NOT to open the *presentation.* It is simply to set you up for YOUR opening. The introduction starts the emotional train moving, it gets them excited about YOU and makes them feel glad that they came to your seminar. The best introduction will have people leaning over to each other whispering *"Wow, this is going to be good!"*

The most critical time...
The opening two minutes

Beyond the introduction, the first two minutes of your seminar are a very important time for generating respect. I want to cover in detail several areas of concern during this opening segment.

Let them drink you in...

The introduction has ended and you begin to move to the podium. Now pause for FOUR SECONDS and don't say anything! This immediately creates a sense of anticipation and drama. This four-second pause will do more to gain control of the room than any words you could say at this point. Also, the first impression is definitely a visual one and you've got to give the audience a chance to look you over. What are they looking for?

Height & Posture

Don't slouch...stand as tall as possible. There are volumes of evidence that suggest that people respect height. If you're already tall, that's fine. If not, don't be afraid to use a riser. This is a four by eight foot covered plywood platform, like a miniature stage roughly 10 inches high.

You can use a riser at the podium or create an entire stage effect with multiple risers in the front of your room. I love risers. They make me feel majestic. One problem with risers is noise — they have a tendency to squeak and wobble when you walk on them which can be distracting. If you're planning to use risers, check them out before starting the seminar.

Dress

Look the part of a successful business professional. How's that for vague advice? We could spend a whole day discussing this area, but I will pay you the courtesy of assuming that you are polished and presentable in your appearance.

As for clothes: one school of thought says you should dress on par with your audience to make them see you as one of them. Others say you should dress to the nines to set yourself apart from the crowd. I have a simple rule for dressing the part — be neat, be clean and be yourself. A pressed suit is the standard dress uniform for both men and women in a public seminar. Beyond that, it's a matter of taste.

If you are one of those "roll-up-your-sleeves" kind of speakers, remember, it's easier to start out looking formal and get more casual as the drama of the meeting and entropy take their toll. Unbuttoning your jacket, even loosening your tie are excellent tools for dramatic effect if used properly, but it's much harder to start casual and dress up as you go.

The goal here is RESPECT. What does the ideal, textbook investment professional look like? Allowing for wide variance in body-type, (and in my case "wide" is the appropriate word), always look professional, clean and crisp. Enough said.

Grab their respect and get control with a...
Powerful opening segment

The first words out of your mouth are critical for gaining emotional momentum with an audience. Choose these words with care and master the delivery of the opener because at no other time will the audience be as open to impression as they are right now. Slow down, take your time, be in control yourself and you will quickly gather control of the room.

There are many ways to open the meeting. Some like using humor, others prefer a dramatic *"let's get right into it"* kind of approach. I will often use a "shocker" or a power sentence that sets a very exciting and dramatic tone. It lets them know that they're in for a very special ride and I've got a firm hand on the tiller.

Depending on the mood you want to create you can start boldly or more relaxed. But whatever you do, be decisive and MEMORIZE the opening. Eye contact is critical. We can debate the merits of speakers who use notes vs. no notes. It doesn't matter if you are planning to read to the crowd from the phone book, the opening must be smooth, controlled and you should deliver it with direct, non-scanning contact.

A "scanner" is someone whose head constantly swivels while talking. They're looking in the general direction of the audience, and it may seem like eye contact, but their eyes are "watering the lawn" with glances that don't linger long enough on any one person for contact to actually be made.

Instead, find a pair of eyes, slow down, focus and deliver an entire thought to that one person. The power is enormous. Not only will that person feel a direct bond with you but people in the immediate vicinity will think you're talking right to them and the effect spreads.

The Basic Opener

Avoid the common, obvious, trite or tiresome opener at all costs. Leave those to your competition. Let the first words out of your mouth carry the impact of a photon torpedo. For example, instead of saying,

"Thanks for coming Ladies & Gentlemen. I'm here tonight to discuss retirement planning..."

Try this — stand silent for four seconds, then begin...

"There are fifty people in this room right now. Twenty years from tonight...forty-six of you will be flat broke, financially dependent on the government, living on food stamps or worse yet...living with your children. Only two

***of you will be completely independent financially. Who
is it going to be?"***

That gets the blood pounding in their ears.

Here is a standard opening for a generic seminar on **"Investing
in the 90's"** as an example. It starts cold...these are literally the first
words that come out of my mouth after I have moved into position
and let the audience look me over in silence for a four count. The
words themselves are spoken with a slow and deliberate pace...almost
as if I'm searching for them individually. The emotional content is
evident. Also, if you're nervous...the opening is where it will show.
Slowing down the pace is not only a very dramatic technique, it helps
keep nerves under control.

***"The vast majority of people today (PAUSE) are
confused and troubled (PAUSE) about this economy.
(PAUSE) They feel bombarded by the media, bullied by
sales people and bewildered by the million things they
need to know to survive in this financial jungle."***

Like that? Bombarded, bullied and bewildered. That's called
alliteration and I'm way too fond of it.

Now the pace picks up a bit and the volume rises...a bit more
strident delivery.

***"Over the past three years they've seen all the
investment lessons they learned in the 80's fail them.
They know they can't live much longer on 5% rates and
yet they're scared, and hesitant to make crucial
decisions. And, to make it worse, right now...90 million
Americans are faced with the most critical investment
challenges of their lives!"***

Pause...let all that sink in for a minute. Make a mini-transition
here.

***"Tonight, we are going to shed some light on this
darkness. We are going to break this problem down and
analyze it carefully. (pause) And when you leave here
(pause), you're going to have a very clear view of the
choices open to you. You're going to feel much more
confident and prepared to meet all the financial goals
you have."***

"Above all, you're going to be a little smarter than when you came in. You're going to understand WHY things happen in the financial world and specifically what you can do about them . . . and we're going to have a little fun in the process. OK . . . let's get right into it."

Notice all the emotional hot buttons we hit — we said people are scared, confused, troubled and hesitant. Then we led them toward confidence, "smart-ness," understanding and fun. This is the whole seminar in a nutshell. In fact, that opening is a microcosm of their entire relationship with you.

Practice your opening until it's smooth and can be delivered with proper emphasis and dramatic flair. If you're going to be monotone and boring, please wait until the body of the presentation. Make the opening powerful!

The Shocker

The shocker is a surprise or unexpected opening. It's not easy to pull off, but when you nail it you can really set an exciting tone for the entire evening. Here's a simple shocker you can use in nearly any seminar:

Walk up to the podium and don't say a word. Once again, pause for a full four seconds. Now, reach into your wallet and pull out a $10 bill.

"Who can tell me where the market closed today?"

Hands will go up, people will laugh. You're giving someone a chance to show off. They assume you're going to give the ten to the person with the correct answer, but you're not.

"Anybody?"

Someone will invariably throw out a number very close or right on the market close. Start walking over to that person, very slowly.

"OK...now who can honestly say they have no idea where the market closed? Be honest?"

More relaxing laughter and someone may raise their hand.

"Excellent!"

Stop...move quickly to that person and give THEM the ten dollars!

"I bet you all thought I was going to give the ten to him."

(point to the person who guessed the close correctly)

"Folks, I've got some news for you...the winners in the world of investing are the people who know and obey the First Rule of the Serious Investor – THINK LONG TERM! If you are constantly watching and worrying about where the Dow Jones Industrial Average closed on any given day YOU ARE DOOMED! That's the first exploded myth of the evening . . . we'll blow up a few more before the night is out!"

Then move into your basic opening.

This kind of opening says this person is a fun, exciting, dynamic and creative speaker. If you're in the audience, you're wide awake and ready to have a great time and learn some stuff you never thought you would learn in your typical boring investment seminar.

There are many forms of the Shocker opening. Another dramatic opener involves the use of props. I love to use money in my opener because it reminds people of exactly why they are there.

Without saying a word, take a dollar bill out of your pocket. Hold it up for the mandatory four-second pause and then begin...

"Do you know what this is?"

Allow five or ten seconds of drama to build. Move ahead slowly.

"You may THINK it's a dollar bill...but it's not. (PAUSE) It's your entire retirement nestegg! All the money you've saved up until the moment you stop working. Here it is! Your IRAs, your 401k, your investments, your pension, Social Security, the equity in your home...everything!"

You've got their attention now.

"At some point in your life...this is what you're going to be living on and the chances are that you want to do everything in your power to protect this money. But let me show you what's happening to this money while you're not looking."

Take out a pair of scissors.

"Every year the nestegg is eroding. Little by little."

Snip off a small corner, then another and another.

"In ten years, more than one third of your total assets will be gone."

Snip off one third of the bill.

"Not because you've bought a vacation home or taken a trip or helped your grandchildren go to college — this money has simply evaporated because of what? (PAUSE) INFLATION."

"I'm only using four percent inflation, not the double digit numbers of the 1980s. After twenty years, you're down to 44 cents on your retirement dollar."

Cut the bill down to 44%.

"Folks, there are two undeniable trends in America today — forces that no one can dispute and that will shape our lives for decades to come. Both have to do with demographics. Part one is that more Americans will retire over the next twenty years then ever before in history putting tremendous strain on programs like Social Security and Medicare. Part two is that we are all living much longer than any generation ever did in the past meaning that our need for income is stretched out now over twenty, thirty and possibly forty more years after retirement."

Take the remaining dollar and cut on the beat.

"We (snip) *are* (snip) *in* (snip) *trouble.* (snip). *And that's why you're here tonight. Let's get started."*

Visual, dramatic, powerful and fun. You have also used very physical concepts in the opening. In fact, what you've done without realizing it is connected with the visual, auditory and kinesthetic sensory reference frames all at once. This is like a three front attack on their minds.

Can anyone think of a way to hit an additional sensory reference frame? I've got a good one...but let's see if you're following me here.

With an opening like this, there's no way they can ignore you even IF they wanted to. You've got their attention. They're excited and under your control.

In short...

Your opening doesn't need to be elaborate or overly dramatic. To create a feeling of respect you simply need to do something different, something exciting, something that shows an audience that you are ready and able to take them on a stimulating and enlightening ride. Find a way that fits your style to open a presentation using some of the techniques we've discussed. You will see immediate results.

Respect is ultimately...
A mental attitude

I think that before you can become a truly effective public seminar presenter you've got to firmly *believe* in your own value — that you are an expert who can truly help solve people's most important financial problems. I recall many times doing seminars with young brokers. They would be nervous and jumpy and all giggly. They couldn't wait to get out there and prove to everyone how young and inexperienced they were.

I wanted to grab them by the collar and shake them. *"Stay focused...you're not some goofy college kid anymore. These people have come to hear you speak about money. This is the time to demonstrate some presence and assume the role of a professional."*

An audience wants to respect you. You're the speaker for Pete's sake. We are conditioned from childhood to respect the person in front of the room...so you're starting with a built-in advantage. All too often, however, we allow our own lack of confidence to show through and this damages the presentation and along with it...your chances for any follow-up.

I'm not saying that you can't be human and natural out there. All I suggest is that your moment in front of an audience must be wrapped in a self-assured, professional demeanor. This is the time to shine. Expect greatness and it will come. Expect failure and guess what?

Lord knows none of us would be in this business if we didn't have a pretty high degree of self-confidence already, but speaking in front of an audience has a way of making you doubt yourself. There's no way around it except to reach down deep inside and draw on those feelings of pride and confidence that got you here. They will not let you down.

Speak as an authority
It's YOU they've come to see

This is a major point that has an impact on both Respect & Confidence. It weaves throughout your seminar. Some of you are going to disagree with my advice. All I can suggest is that you try it and see the results for yourself.

When you stand in front of a room and give a presentation, you have a lot of people behind you — invisible people but critical to your success nonetheless. People like economists, market strategists, portfolio managers, experts and geniuses who make the big calls.

Their insights may be very valuable in the creation of your presentation — BUT — in a seminar, every thought out of your mouth should be YOURS. Unless you are specifically referencing another professional's work, you own all the opinions, the theories, the advise...everything.

Your goal is to get the audience to buy YOU...not the rocket scientists back in New York or the unseen market gurus who give YOU advice. Those experts are not here doing the seminar. They are not the ones who will have to take the concerned phone calls when the market drops or hold hands through tough times or convince a reluctant client to take action that's clearly in their best interest.

Yes...you want the audience to know that you're part of a greater whole. You want them to understand that you have a team of experts on your staff backing you up in case you need help. But YOU are the cog in this wheel and everything revolves around you.

It all comes down to very subtle attitude shifts in the way you present material. Let me give you an example. Here are two ways to say the same thing. How do you feel about them?

— 1 —

"My firm believes that Inflation is not likely to be a problem over the next four to six years. Our Chief Economist, Dr. I. C. Dimly is calling for two percent through the end of the decade."

— 2 —

"Everything I've seen indicates to me that inflation is going to be roughly two percent over the next several years. Economist consensus bears this out and all the data shows that inflation is well under control."

The difference in the words is slight, but it leads to a major difference in how you are perceived by the audience.

Version #1 alludes to a Chief Economist and "your firm." Your role in this inflation analysis is that of a reporter, not an independent thinker. With #2, you are in the center of the process. The "everything" you may have seen is the exact same report from the Chief Economist, but the *way you're saying it now* implies that YOU understand and can reason through complex economic analysis. It creates a whole different picture — one that yields very powerful results when it comes to building relationships and your overall business.

You have a right and an *obligation* to impress the audience with your knowledge and ability. Attributing an expert's work is fine...and I'm absolutely NOT saying that you should claim credit for the ideas and effort of others. But we live in a great big universe of information. In our industry, reality is fleeting and truths change every day. In the midst of this confusion, the audience must believe that you are much more than just a spokesperson or an observer — you are a thinker with your own set of beliefs and analytical tools.

Using guest speakers

Many financial advisors do seminars with guest speakers like a product wholesaler or portfolio manager. I have no problem with these events. I've done hundreds of them myself and they can enhance your image as a "connected" professional IF you do them right. But too many advisors simply stand up and say *"Hi everyone. Thanks for coming. Here's Joe Expert."* and then they sit around a month later swearing that seminars don't work.

You're still in control

No matter how important or dynamic your guest speaker may be — YOU must be in control of the seminar if you expect to do any business from the event. You should position the guest speaker as a specialist or expert who works for you. They are part of the "team" backing you up. If possible, have the speaker say something nice about you after you introduce them:

"Thank you Frank. Ladies and gentlemen, I'm very happy to be here tonight. Frank & I have worked closely together for a number of years now and I'm always thrilled to come to Denver to share some ideas with his clients."

You want to make people think that you're the center of a solar system of experts and specialists and that you have the power to deliver these experts to your clients.

Open, close & Q&A

You must deliver the opening and closing segments of the seminar. Discuss this with your guest. They know you need to establish audience control and they might suggest a powerful opener or close that meshes well with their talk. Avoid repeating part of your guest's message or stealing his opener. That could throw him off track if he's not prepared.

There are two ways to conduct a Q&A session with a guest speaker. You can become an active participant answering questions side by side with your guest or you can be a facilitator for the process.

If the presentation involves complex subjects and you've positioned the guest as the expert, you probably don't want to jump in with your two cents on every question. Let them do their job while you simply make sure the process goes smoothly. If the talk was on a less technical level — where you could be expected to have some knowledge, then it's OK to jump in. Please avoid the tendency to give long answers. The feeling may be...

"Hey, this is a question I can answer...now it's my turn to show everyone how much I know."

This is a sure sign of insecurity.

You're still the "product" they must "buy"

Make no mistake. Having a guest speaker conduct the bulk of your seminar is much less effective from a business standpoint than doing it yourself. Every wholesaler has had the uncomfortable experience of doing a great seminar for a broker and having people in the audience come up to them afterwards wanting the wholesaler to handle their account.

It's not a good feeling knowing that these prospects are never going to do business with the broker who invited you because the broker didn't sell himself to the audience in any way.

As brilliant as your guest speakers may be, YOU are the person who makes it all come together for the CLIENT. The need to exude confidence and professionalism is even higher now that you're not the main speaker. That's the only hope you have of convincing the crowd to do business with you.

Your final goal in doing seminars with guest specialists should be to get good enough to do your own seminars as quickly as possible. Borrow their techniques and learn from them. Chances are they've developed some strong presentation skills that you can modify to fit your style and use in your own seminars.

What about
"Tag Team" seminars

Many of you will be tempted to join forces with others in your firm to do a seminar. On the surface, this seems like a great way to share the work load and the cost of the event. Each of you brings a set of skills to the process and you can synergize to produce even greater results than either could alone.

My experience has been quite the opposite. Rarely, in fact, do these "partnerships" work. The collapse can come from several structural weaknesses. Often a senior colleague will take a rookie "under his wing" to do a seminar together. Can you guess who is going to do the work and who is going to reap the rewards?

I would avoid these kinds of team-ups like the plague. Even when both partners are comparative equals, one is always more committed to the event and inevitably resents the other for "just showing up" and putting forth little or no effort.

Add to these problems the fact that both of you have different presentation styles. The audience is going to have to get comfortable with two delivery methods, two senses of humor, two levels of energy.

The bottom line in my opinion, is that teams don't work when it comes to seminars. I feel very strongly that seminars are a one-man show where you control every aspect of the "sales presentation" of yourself as the product. Now I know there are exceptions to every rule, and if you're in a partnership that's doing top-quality seminars, then just forget what I'm saying.

CHAPTER 7

CONFIDENCE

"Confidence is a plant of slow growth in an aged bosom."

William Pitt Earl of Chatham

T HERE ARE TWO KINDS OF CONFIDENCE you need to generate during an investment seminar. First, is confidence in YOU. You want the audience to trust your judgment and expertise. On a fundamental level, they need to know that you have the professional tools that can help solve their problems. On a deeper level, you want to give them confidence in you personally as someone who knows the ins and outs of your industry better than other advisors.

The second kind of confidence may seem a little strange, but you want them to develop more confidence in themselves. You want them to trust their own judgment just enough to feel good about coming to you and about accepting high quality advice. After all, what good is it if you're the best advisor in the nation if your clients can't recognize it or appreciate it due to their own lack of investment confidence. What am I talking about?

If you generate confidence only in your ability and judgment, there's a good chance that they may not have sufficient trust in themselves to even set an appointment with you. They may think they need to learn more about the markets or wait until they have more money before they can seek your help. They may even fear placing too much confidence in any one advisor and stay away entirely.

Making them more confident investors makes them better, happier clients. They will feel good about themselves and more secure in their own abilities with you as their partner. That's the ideal situation.

Let's start with you. You generate confidence in yourself essentially by what you say and how you say it. Through these elements, you display a depth of knowledge about your profession, understanding about the implications of investment actions and an empathy for their real life concerns.

What do I say?
Start with knowledge

The basis of the entire seminar process is the fact that you KNOW SOMETHING. You are an expert in investing, maybe with a specialty in some particular branch, it doesn't matter. All that matters for our purposes, is that you have something intelligent to say — a message of some importance and insight. Otherwise, why are you doing seminars at all?

By the way, I would never presume to tell you what to say. Each of you has his or her own philosophy about investing, the economy and what to do about it. The message you choose to send to an audience must be based on the kind of business you do and on what YOU believe is best for your clients.

The content of your seminar is entirely up to you, but given that you do have a message, there are two things that will make your seminar different and more powerful than those of other financial professionals:

- The organization of your thoughts
- The style of your delivery

The structure of how you present ideas and the way you say what you say is every bit as important as the ideas themselves. I could easily make the case that it's MORE important.

We talked about organization of the seminar in the chapter on UNDERSTANDING. Now you need to realize that the better organized you are, the more confidence you will generate in the minds of the audience.

To the degree that you can present a logical flow of ideas leading to a viable conclusion, the audience is much more likely to believe you. If you jump around from thought to thought without establishing a firm foundation upon which to build your case, the audience will reject your conclusions and lose confidence in your abilities.

As for delivery, there are certain techniques you can use to enhance the message being delivered. This will also raise the audience's confidence in you. Use them, and you will be more believable — it's that simple.

The building blocks of
A confident presentation

There are five main construction materials you have available when you're building a seminar. These are:

- Opinions
- Facts & Factoids
- Statistics
- Stories
- Quotes

The basic way you put these together goes like this:

You start with OPINIONS:

"There is a coming retirement crisis in America! Millions of people are facing the toughest financial decisions of their lives and they are not prepared."

Backed-up by FACTS:

"There are over 76 million Baby Boomers who will be facing retirement starting in the year 2010. Imagine this...the largest demographic group in U.S. history all drawing Social Security at the same time."

Enhanced by STATISTICS:

"According to the Bureau of Labor Statistics, when Social Security began, there were 35 workers supporting each retiree. By the time the Baby Boomers are all over 65, that number will be down to two workers for each retiree."

Dramatized by QUOTES:

"Richard Darman, the controversial and far-thinking budget director under George Bush, described this situation in very dramatic terms — 'The retirement crisis this nation faces in the next decade will change forever the way Americans think about investing and saving. It will have an economic and emotional impact on this nation far deeper than the Great Depression of the 1930's.'"

Personalized by STORIES:

"I just began working with a new client about a month ago. We'll call him Bob. He's fifty years old with a wife and three kids. He's worked for the same company for twenty years and he's begun to think about retirement. So, he came in one evening and we did a complete analysis of his financial situation...including projected costs for college and the possibility that he'd have to take care of an elderly parent. (Which are expenses faced by over 60% of Baby Boomers.) Let me give you an idea of the numbers we came up with."

"To generate an annual income of $90,000 which is only 70% of his current income, Bob would have to put away over $3,800 a month for the next 15 years! That includes his company pension AND social security and presumes his kids go to a state college. God forbid they get into Harvard or Cal Tech...his monthly number jumps up to $6,300 a month!"

I offer this segment as an illustration of the logical underpinnings of a theme. Everyone has an opinion. That leaves you with four basic "knowledge tools" that you can use to generate confidence in any public presentation — facts, statistics, quotes and stories. The audience expects you, as an expert in your field and someone to whom they will entrust their assets, to demonstrate your knowledge and ability with some compelling combination of these tools.

The bricks and mortar
Fact & statistics

Accurate, pertinent and carefully articulated facts form the base of your discussion. They are the "meat" of the seminar. They are what will appeal to the audience's logical side. And even though we're focused on emotion, you cannot ignore their logical side.

People today like to think of themselves as logical investors. Whether that's true or not is open for debate. But I promise that if you walk into a seminar armed only with weakly supported opinions and expect to sway the crowd on the force of your presence alone, you're crazy. It will not work. They want hard facts...numbers and "proof."

The good news is that you can find facts and statistics to prove just about any damn thing you want. Wall Street suffers from data overload. I guarantee that you can find support for any opinion you may have, given a little legwork.

Frame the picture

Facts, data and statistics by themselves are dry, unemotional things. Used in an ordinary fashion, they are low impact items that often clutter and confuse a presentation. Most speakers deliver them in a very boring style. Instead, make them come alive by framing or packaging them with an introduction and a meaningful interpretation.

Facts and statistics are only valuable in their ability to carry or illustrate a powerful emotional message. It's the emotional impact of the data that you must highlight. For example, you're about to quote a fact and a supporting statistic. You can simply blurt it out and let it hang there or you can deliver it properly like this:

Part 1: The Fact:
"The best performing investment throughout history (PAUSE) has been stocks."

Part 2: The Frame:
"That may not surprise some of you but let me give you some data to support that fact. This statistic comes from Ibbottson. They are the resource data bank that all of Wall Street turns to for statistical information."

Part 3. The Statistic:
"According to Ibbottson, the average return on the S&P 500 over the past 65 years has been 10.5% per year!"

Part 4: Repeat and Spin
"Ten point five percent per year compounded since 1928...sixty eight years of double digit growth! Nothing else even comes close. And that's the S&P 500, not a

select group of aggressive growth stocks or an actively managed portfolio. The S&P is just a broad index of big companies — some very good others not so good."

Part 5: Why is this important?

"Think about what this means. It's a simple statistic but it forms the base for our entire talk tonight. No other investment you can find will help you grow your assets faster or more consistently than stocks. I can show you numbers back to 1926 but just go back ten years and you would have nearly TRIPLED your asset base!"

Part 6: Connection & Transition

"Now that's all just fine in a vacuum, but we don't invest in a vacuum. How does that performance compare to other investments you might make – bonds, for example? I said stocks were number one performing asset class and that nothing else comes close." (PAUSE)

Part 3 Again: The Connecting Statistic

"Bonds, during that same period of time, were #2 but with an average of only 4.5%! That's less than half the annual return on stocks."

Using a powerful statistic without a proper frame leaves the audience alone to try and find the meaning. This isn't a mystery novel...TELL them the meaning in plain, emotional language. Tell them where the statistic comes from and how respectable Ibbottson is in our industry. Then quote it in a semi-dramatic fashion with proper delivery and emphasis. Then repeat it and add a new interpretation. Then make it relate to them in real dollar terms. Then connect it to the next point in your discussion.

You've created life from lifelessness.

If you've got several facts and stats to use in one segment of your presentation, it's not necessary to frame and repeat each one. Instead, let them build to a natural climax and then summarize them with an emotional interpretation. For example:

"You've now seen the demographic chart that shows Americans are living longer than at any other time in history. You saw the numbers on Social Security and the savings rate and I showed you the statistics on the average investor's returns."

"All of this adds up to a powerful message — if we keep going the way we're headed, none of us will not be able to afford retirement!"

This approach to facts and statistics takes them out of the realm of the ordinary and places them into the exciting position they deserve. And with this approach, you don't need a lot of them.

I said facts and stats were the "meat" of the seminar. Well carry this food analogy further. If you think of a seminar as a meal, to overload them on facts and stats is like serving six courses of steak and beef and chicken and sausage. All that meat will make them sick. Too many facts and stats will bloat their brains and they'll slip quickly into a mental digestive coma.

You've seen this a hundred times. Your firm's Chief Brainiac gets up in front of a room and does a core dump of every arcane techno-tidbit he's uncovered in the past six months. The audience is lost somewhere after the third scattergram. *Mission failure!*

The best seminars I've given or seen were based on one main theme supported by a small handful of facts and solid statistics. Even allowing for the fact that the public has gotten smarter, this is still all you need to create a seminar that will knock their socks off and have them calling you for an appointment.

Too many facts and statistics can even make an audience angry after a while. They will shut down mentally and begin to resent you for NOT creating an emotional argument as to why all of this is important to them. Meanwhile, you're up there diagramming the history of the Universe thinking you're doing a fantastic seminar, and they're looking for the nearest exit.

Once upon a time...
Tell them a story

Humans have used stories to convey important emotional messages since the dawn of time. We like stories on a conscious and sub-conscious level. They fit into our reality in a way which facts and statistics cannot.

There are three basic stories you should use in a seminar: the horror story, the docu-drama and the celebrity confession.

The horror story

The horror story illustrates what happened to someone who didn't follow your advice or who made a decision based on an assessment of the facts that conflicted with your recommendation. It can be a tale of investor woe, a dramatic error in judgement made by others, a sad or scary event that caused someone to lose a fortune. You've probably heard a million of them and participated in a few yourself. Here's an example:

> *"Folks, I'm not the smartest guy in the world, but I can spot trouble a mile away. When I was a broker back in Baltimore in 1983, I had a client named Dorothy."*
>
> *"One day she called me and told me to liquidate her account. I asked 'Why? What happened?' She had a solid portfolio of blue chip companies, nothing too exciting, but a good portfolio."*
>
> *"She said she was going to put all her money in CDs at the local savings and loan. 'The rates are fantastic!' she said. I told her, 'Dorothy, no one can offer you 13% on a guaranteed investment...it's just not possible!' "*
>
> *"She insisted, so I let her go. (PAUSE) You all know what happened to Savings & Loans back in the 80s. She is still waiting for her principal from those CDs."*
>
> *"The moral of that story is simple — there are no guarantees."*

Is this too transparent? Well, maybe. But it plays very well in front of a crowd of people who are likely to think that banks are the safest place to stash their money.

The docu-drama

This is like a re-enactment designed to give them an inside look at some great moment in financial history. It simultaneously adds weight to your theme and illustrates that you have taken the time to study your craft (something that far too few financial professionals ever do).

My favorite docu-drama stars Lyndon Johnson, Jimmy Hoffa & Ronald Reagan. I use it to show how labor costs affect inflation. You can dispute the conclusions, but you cannot dispute the powerful effect this story has on an audience. They love it!

"Let me set the scene. The year is 1968. A conference room in the White House. At one end of the table, President Lyndon Johnson. At the other end of the table, (PAUSE) Jimmy Hoffa!"

"Now who was Jimmy Hoffa in 1968? (PAUSE) President of the Teamsters Union. Arguably the most powerful union leader in the nation. Hoffa had a feud with Johnson that dated back into Kennedy's administration. He pounded the table . . .

(pound the table)
and said, 'Mr. Johnson, I'm going to close this country down in three days!'."

"Well, Hoffa had the power. He controlled the Teamsters and unions, (2 beat PAUSE) UNIONS controlled 37% of the labor force in 1968. If he said 'strike' he COULD have closed the country down! Johnson had to back down."

(Pause and take your time for the story to sink in. The crowd is loving this. It's history come alive. By the way, did you notice that factoid I threw in there? Very casually, as if I was born knowing detailed labor market statistics.)

"Now, come forward in time to 1981. The same room in the White House. At this end of the table, (PAUSE) President Ronald Reagan. And at the other end...President of the Air Traffic Controller Union! Does this ring any bells?"

(Some people will see where you're headed with this story and the excitement will start to build.)

"The ATC President tried to do his best Jimmy Hoffa impersonation. He pounded the table and said, 'Mr. Reagan, we are going to close this country's airports down in 24 hours! We're going on strike!'"

(PAUSE — people will remember this event and you'll see the spark of recognition in their eyes. They're really getting into it! Which is exactly what you want!)

"Ronald Reagan said 'No! You can't go on strike. If you go on strike, you're fired!'."

"Well that was a hollow threat. How could anyone fire the Air Traffic Controllers? These aren't truck drivers.

There are only 22,000 of them. It takes three years to BECOME an Air Traffic Controller!"

"So, they went on strike (PAUSE) and what did Ronald Reagan do? (PAUSE) He fired them! Not only did he fire them but he LOCKED THEM OUT! If you were an Air Traffic Controller who went on strike you could never be an Air Traffic Controller again!"

"Why is this important? Well, Ronald Reagan sent a powerful message to organized labor in this country. He ushered in the most anti-labor administration in the history of the U.S. Union representation declined from 37% of the workforce to BELOW 15%. Today, in a globally competitive market, when a union goes to the bargaining table they have virtually no ability to argue for (PAUSE — slow and soft) higher wages."

"Why is this important to YOU? Sixty five percent of inflation is labor cost. If you can keep labor costs under control you can whip inflation."

Delivered well, this story ignites a fire of confidence in them that only years of poor advice will extinguish. You've tied two historical events together in such a way as to illustrate a major global economic trend. For the first time, many of them will understand the big picture — all because of you.

One more thing — if you can't find a story from your own life experience that fits your theme — get one from someplace else and make it yours. Take a story from a magazine or newspaper. I pick them up from every source imaginable. One story I used for years came from National Geographic Magazine. It was about the fires in Kuwait set by Saddam Hussein. It provided a good proof source and visual aid for part of my low inflation scenario.

The celebrity confession

The celebrity confession is a simple story designed to link you with a mover and a shaker in the financial industry. Use these carefully because they can easily be perceived as mere name dropping if they don't fit your theme or are delivered in too grand a fashion. I almost prefer them as a "throw-away" or "aside."

Stories that link you directly or indirectly with top portfolio managers and regional business leaders all lend energy to your aura. Usually it's best to simplify and boil down such stories to their essence.

A few years ago during the big oil boom in the U.S., I attended a huge luncheon at which the guest speaker was T. Boone Pickens. Now there were well over a thousand people at this luncheon, but for years after that, whenever the subject of oil or gas came up in a seminar or in any conversation, my story would begin with,

"There I was...having lunch with T. Boone Pickens..."

It was completely true. He was there...I was there. We were both eating lunch. I saw no reason to go further.

The art is in the telling

A story is a very emotional tool. You've got to tell it as if you were there...with all the fervor of an actual participant. Try to imagine yourself or your clients at the very center of the drama. Doing this makes the story come alive for your audience and carries more weight and emotional impact than coldly relating a third-party event.

The stories you tell and the way you tell them can have an audience believing that Alan Greenspan personally calls you up for advice on interest rates. Here's where good acting skills will help make a major impact on your seminar.

Someone once said...
Quotes

Quotes give legitimacy and strength to your theme that other knowledge tools can't match. They can add the credibility of a third party to your own stature and can reflect current mainstream thinking on a particular subject.

I like to quote two types of sources — the well-known and the unknown. I will quote big names like Peter Lynch or Alan Greenspan or from articles appearing in the Wall Street Journal, The Times, Business Week, Forbes and the like. These are people and publications that your audience knows and EXPECTS you to know too. *I used to quote Dan Dorfmann, but now I use him as a celebrity confession.*

Then I'll come right back with the Chairman of the District Federal Reserve Bank, a corporate CEO, a foreign government official or a Wall Street analyst. I'll mention things I saw in The Economist, Lancet, Harvard Business Review and Institutional Investor — someone the audience has never heard of or a publication they are not likely to read.

"Why," you ask, *"quote someone they never heard of or some article they've never seen. What good is that?"*

This is important and it ties in with the celebrity confession...

Your clients and prospects want to think that you're connected. They want their financial advisor to be part of the game, a real "insider." It gives them a thrill to tell their friends, *"My advisor had dinner with Warren Buffett (or lunch with T. Boone Pickens). Oh he knows everybody!"* It makes them feel important too.

They are really impressed when you can move beyond the celebrities and drop names of the real power insiders. The President of Ecuador or the Director of the Congressional Budget Office or the CEO of British Petroleum are not known by the average or even the pseudo-sophisticated investor. You have now jumped two notches in their minds and you've found an ideal factoid to support your message.

There is another huge advantage to referencing semi-obscure individuals or studies. If you think about it for a minute it will come to you! If not - just answer this question. Ten pages ago I quoted Richard Darden, President Bush's Budget Director. Now you're in the business right, so you probably have heard of Dick Darman. But if I used the same words without quoting someone like Darman, would it have carried the same weight?

These kinds of "obscure" quotes and factoids can be a compelling tool, especially in a world like ours where every opinion is equally meaningful or meaningless and facts are fleeting, wispy things. Find the ones that support your story and that make sense to you and use them to add spice to your overall presentation.

"Hey wait just a minute here. Are you saying I should control the dissemination of data and supporting facts to favor and strengthen the presentation of my own investment ideas and themes?

Give that man a Macanudo!

Folks, absolutely no one ever said to make stuff up or alter the facts. That's just plain dumb. Simply keep digging and researching until you FIND support for your ideas. Barring the most outlandish ideas, this should be easy.

They're small but powerful
Factoids

Unlike facts, stories, quotes and statistics which form the basis of the entire presentation, factoids are little bits of information that you can sprinkle throughout your presentation. They're intelligent "bursts of precision" that support your emotional message and give the audience the impression that you are extremely comfortable with the main and related topics.

To find them, you can reference surveys, research reports, articles, or any of the thousand data sources at our disposal.

Use them in a very relaxed style. Try to make them almost a subliminal tool rather than an overt one. For example, you'll be talking about growth in foreign markets and inject a factoid about Indonesia being the fourth largest country in the world with nearly two hundred million people.

Do it in a very off-hand manner in what actor's call a "throw-away" because you want them to believe that you're so conversant about Indonesia that this kind of stuff comes out of your mouth all day long. Scatter these gems throughout the body of your presentation and use them in your Teaching Take-Aways, which we will discuss later.

When it comes to stuff they already know...
Tell them the truth

The simplest technique I've ever seen for developing a sense of confidence from a group of total strangers is an advanced concept called the TRUTH!

I will often discuss specific issues that others might try to avoid, like RISK and FEES. These are two great concerns of every investor, yet many advisors try to ignore them or sweep them under a rug. Do the opposite — highlight them!

Look, you're not going to tell them anything they don't already know. Every investment has risk and every investment has some sort of fee or else we wouldn't be here. Why hide from it? Instead, hit it right on the head very openly and honestly.

Clients know from experience that many brokers and financial advisors are not eager to talk about sensitive subjects like risk, commissions or fees. And they're right! Is it any surprise that risk and commissions are nearly always the unspoken objection in the investment sales process. Why we're afraid to talk about it is beyond my understanding, so I use this incredulity to my advantage.

"Folks, I want to talk about something that I suspect is very important to you — the fees for investing. All these great strategies I've outlined for you — what will they cost to implement? How do commissions work? What are your options and which method may actually be more expensive in both the long- and short-term?"

"I've found that many people don't really know how they pay for professional advice or how much the fees are on various investments. I suppose this shouldn't surprise me since most brokers would rather take out their own appendix with a rusty spoon than talk about commissions, but I'd like to touch on this briefly, is this of interest to anyone?"

One thousand seminars and I've never heard "NO."

In my experience, commissions and risk are the two most trust-generating things you can talk about. You would be amazed to know how few "civilians" understand what they're paying for various investments or what the real downside is in an investment program. The only source of commission or risk information they have is the media — the evil, malignant destroyer of trust between advisor and client. *"Never let your worst enemy control the thoughts of your clients."* Remember **The Art of War** by Sun Tsu? Well this is a direct quote from **The Art of Sales** by Sun Stu, his distant cousin and famous 3rd Century Chinese customer's man.

Whereas commissions can be a topic all to themselves, risk can be woven into every phase of a discussion of investment ideas. Focus very directly because you want them to know that you don't hide risk from them and that you understand how important their money is. Also, you want them to believe that you're better, smarter, more honest and have a deeper understanding of risk than the typical financial advisor.

The second potential benefit of discussing risk and fees is that you reduce the threat of the unknown. You shine a light on the demon and often, it just goes away. Neither risk nor fees are often as bad as the public thinks, so by bringing up the subject first, you have the chance to disarm the objection.

Take care here, however. You don't want to initiate your discussion of fees or risk by saying *"They're not as bad as you think."* First, that will only serve to galvanize opposition. Second, you don't really know what they think yet. Instead, lead them into the discussion professionally and seriously, displaying as much concern as they would...even more! Then, move them slowly toward an enlightened understanding of the topic.

A real confidence builder
The Listerine Sell

If you tell someone a negative thing about yourself they will nearly always believe you. If you follow it up with something positive — they will believe that too!

Listerine used to have an ad campaign that said, *"TASTES TERRIBLE . . . but it works!"* This is a valuable tool to use in a seminar, and here's an example:

"I've got to tell you (PAUSE) I couldn't pick a good stock if it came up and bit me on the nose. But I do know how to find the best money managers in the world."

No one does everything well and everyone appreciates a person who is honest about their strengths and weaknesses. Make this work for you. You can't be all things to all people, so pick something they don't need, (i.e., expertise in commodities or options) and make that your "weakness."

Don't use it too often in one seminar or it will become obvious. Instead, save it for a point of critical discussion, a transition moment where you want to give the feeling of "opening up to the audience," or as a "bonding" human frailty in a moment of self-revelation.

Make it look easy
Sagan on the Cosmos

Confidence goes hand in hand with understanding. These two emotional states blend very well together and lift you to a higher plane in the mind of the audience.

I think of myself as the Wall Street version of Carl Sagan. He was one of the world's top space scientists, renowned for his work on the Voyager planetary probes and his book "Cosmos." But the major reason he was considered to be so good is because he made the complex and arcane worlds of astrophysics and exobiology fun and understandable to the average person.

It's great to to know a lot about our business. Much more prized is the person who can translate our business into understandable language for the common man. In front of the public, you can be the expert who makes the most difficult concepts seem almost mundane. The proper intensity of this style will leave your audience feeling that you are what I call "friendly-smart" — that is an extremely bright individual who doesn't condescend or make others feel like a fool.

Don't be afraid to give them...
Confidence in themselves

The way to give them self-confidence is to teach them something that will make them better investors WITHOUT using an advisor. In this way you make them feel good about their own abilities to meet their financial goals. You empower them just enough to take control of their financial future, but again, not so much that they think they can go it alone.

Clearly, you can't go too far here, because the main purpose of the seminar is to get them to come to you. So I recommend a little technique called the **"Teaching Take-Away."**

Step One of the Teaching Take-Away is where you actually teach them something. You give them a skill set or a piece of knowledge they could use completely on their own (if they had to) to make better decisions about their money. We discussed teaching techniques in the chapter on Understanding.

Step Two is the Take-Away. Having given them a taste of this godly knowledge you must now snatch it back from them and by doing so reinforce the feeling that *"You are the expert — they need your help!"*

You execute the "take-away" by combining a basic teaching point with one or two unexplained factoids, a piece of jargon or a specific situation that's too complex for them to grasp.

For example: you may be talking about the yield curve and describing how rates have declined over the past several years. As a throw-away factoid you may say something like

> *"This all works just fine with a normal, positively sloped curve but if we slip into an inversion...all bets are off."*

What did you say? You used a phrase that fits your yield curve discussion and makes sense to an investment pro but has virtually no meaning to them. By sprinkling one or two of these kinds of phrases at the end of a teaching point you leave them with just a little confusion and awe, enough to get them thinking...

"Wow, just when I thought I understood everything he was saying he proves that he knows a whole lot more than I ever will. I need expert advice!"

Another favorite I used in my global seminars had virtually no meaning but simply sounded great and made me appear as if I knew some inside story that they weren't privy to. I said...

> *"If I see Soros doing any short covering, I'm going long Deutsch Marks just for some protection...at least until the hedges are busted."*

That's borderline doublespeak...but it serves its purpose. Look, I know most of you are too forthright to use techniques like this but let me use a sports analogy to illustrate this point.

Imagine for a minute that you are tennis superstar Pete Sampras and you're playing an exhibition pro-am match with some local club pro who *thinks* he's really good. Tell the truth...don't you blow one or two serves by him just to keep him in his place? Of course you do!

The "Teaching Take-Away" may sound complex or too contrived, but with practice, you can deliver it with ease. In so doing, you're simultaneously giving them tremendous value, high quality content and you're reinforcing their confidence in you. If you're going to use this technique, be certain to stick to take-away concepts that *you* thoroughly understand...just in case there's a sniper out there looking for a clear shot at your credibility.

Written materials help them
Believe in you

We talked earlier about handouts. One of the most powerful confidence builders you can use is to give them stuff written by you. These might be articles, newsletters, white papers, reprints of interviews or any other document that came out of your head.

By the way, what do you think is the number one method used by financial professionals for getting new accounts? Give up?

Write a book!

If you've got the expertise, the writing ability and the time...do it! There may be no better single thing you could do for your business that sets you apart from the crowd as an unassailable expert. I will tell you that it's harder than you might think, but as long as you stick with something you know really well, you might be surprised to realize how much fun it can be.

And no one says you've got to have a book done by tomorrow. This is a project that you can take years to complete. It's taken me five years to get this book to the point you see it today...and it's still not done. There will always be more information in your head than you can put onto paper. You will forever be coming up with new and exciting ways of explaining things. Getting your book into the hands of your potential client base can lead to tremendous success on local and even national levels.

Generate confidence by...
Mastering the Q & A session

One of the best ways to instill confidence in an audience is by adroitly handling the question and answer session. This is a very important process with a dynamic all its own and we'll cover it in complete detail in the chapter on Q&A.

CHAPTER 8

HAPPINESS

"There is no happiness where there is no wisdom."
Sophocles

"The thirst after happiness is never extinguished in the heart of man."
Jean Jacques Rousseau

H UMAN BEINGS ARE OBSESSED BY HAPPINESS. Americans so badly need to feel happy all the time that the founding fathers put it into our Declaration of Independence..."Life, liberty and the pursuit of happiness!"

It's gotten much worse in recent years. People today want to be constantly stimulated toward pleasure of some kind. Nearly every audience you will address in your seminar efforts has one main goal — HAVE A GOOD TIME!

Sure, they want to learn something about their money...but I promise you they don't want to work too hard to do it. They have too much on their minds to sit for an hour listening to some "expert" drone on and on about investments. This is why I say that a good portion, upwards of 70%, of any investment seminar is

Entertainment!

The good news is that you can provide lots of valuable content and STILL be very entertaining. In fact, learning and entertainment go together very well. People love to learn stuff. Our very genes make us insatiably curious and we strive to gather knowledge throughout our lives. But if that knowledge comes attached to an evening of boring economic statistics delivered in a dry and non-compelling manner...it's no longer fun and it will have little impact on their lives. Worse yet, it will generate little business for you.

Investment seminars, therefore, present a dual-edged emotional dilemma when it comes to happiness. Side One goes like this:

"I know I need to learn more about my money. Going to this seminar will provide me with knowledge that could have a direct impact on the quality of my life. It may make me richer or make my family more secure. It can make me seem really smart in the eyes of friends and colleagues at the office. It will give me an intellectual "ticket" to the "big game" where important people make important things happen. I can't wait to get there and I'm confident that this will be a great experience!"

Part Two is a little different.

"I know I need to learn more about my money, but I could be home watching Seinfeld or The Discovery Channel, or playing with my kids, or playing golf, or eating dinner or, or, or. So why in God's name am I going to drive twenty minutes to hear a boring economics lecture from some guy who's going to put me to sleep, try to sell me something I don't want or call me every week at dinner time for a whole year. And besides, Money Magazine said that I can double my money in three years and THAT will make me happy."

There you have the conflict in a nutshell. What will make me more happy, being at an investment seminar or being at home? And if I do go to the seminar, what will make me happy about being there and glad I came? The audience's pursuit of happiness is the critical equation in the whole process. If you can make them happy, you will have accomplished a major mission in the war for their hearts and minds.

So, just how do you make an audience happy?

Two ways:

1. Give them the knowledge they are seeking.

2. Give it to them in a way that's fun and stimulating.

Easy to list but harder to do than would seem at first glance, so let me complicate this for you a bit.

Give them
Knowledge

This is the baseline minimum expectation for the event. You can assume that they responded to your seminar invitation because something in the title or discussion piqued their curiosity. They want information and their desire is fairly straightforward. If you're doing a seminar on annuities, they're not there to hear about stock option financing. So the basic knowledge part of a seminar is not too hard to figure out.

I like to deal with the knowledge issue right up front...very close to the introduction segment of the seminar. I don't want them wondering IF they're going to get the knowledge they came for.

"Folks, I have three main goals for our discussion tonight. You may have some as well and I want to get those out on the table, but first let me tell you what I'd like to accomplish tonight. When you leave here tonight this is what you're going to know:"

"You're going to understand interest rates, what makes them move and the effect their movements have on the economy."

"You're going to understand the major forces that are driving the stock market today AND tomorrow. Which industries are poised for growth and why."

"And finally (remember, only three things) you're going to have a much clearer picture of what to do with your money. In the midst of all this confusion and noise, you're going to have a solid strategy...not a perfect one because nothing is perfect, but a strong gameplan that will get you closer to your goals. How does that sound?"

"Oh...and goal number four is to have some fun. You work too hard to sit and listen to a boring economics lecture for two hours, so we're going to do things a little differently than you may have seen in other seminars."

"Now are there any things that I've missed that you would like to cover tonight?"

If you heard this how would you feel? You would probably be excited and filled with positive expectations. That makes people happy. It gets their juices flowing. They start to get happy about what they're *going* to learn and the fun their *going* to have before you hit one word of seminar content.

If they have issues they want you to cover, go ahead and include them as long as they don't stray too far from the topic. As you know, I advocate maintaining audience control over participation, especially early in the event. So don't get too wrapped up in asking what *they* want to hear. Chances are you're going to cover everything and more.

Beyond basic knowledge
They want dirt

In addition to the basic textbook knowledge that comprises the heart of your seminar...is there anything else an audience wants to know? You bet your boots there is...they want dirt. I'm talking ***Hard Copy***, ***Inside Edition***, ***20/20***, ***60 Minutes***, ***Rescue 911***, ***Cops*** and ***Lifestyles of the Rich & Famous*** all rolled into one!

People love to think that they're getting an "insider's look" at the world of money. They want you to escort them behind the door into that back room where they KNOW the real money is being made. It's just the way we are...there's no reason to fight it. I suggest you go with the flow and build specific items into your presentation that are designed to give them this "secret" information. In fact, I'll bet if you did a seminar entitled:

Secret Stuff That Has Been Known Only To A Handful of Super-Successful Investors And Has Been Kept Hidden From You Until Now!

you would be turning people away at the door. I may do one just to see.

The first way to do this is to actually give them a look behind the door by telling them things known only to financial professionals. One of my favorites is the infamous **Wall Street Week Debunk**. I'll save it for a moment when I want to shift the tone of the event or give them a mental break. It goes like this:

"Folks...let me just take a second for a little tirade here. We've been talking about sources of investment

ideas...where to get them and who is reliable. We haven't talked about television...and for a very good reason. How many of you watch Wall Street Week with Lou Rukeyser?"

Several hands always go up. It's one of the most popular shows on TV.

"That's fine...but let me give you a little unsolicited advice. Please PLEASE remember one thing when you watch that show. No one who appears there, not Frank Cappiello or Marty Zweig or any of the Elves gets paid to give out free investment advice on television. These are all professionals who are paid by clients to give THEM advice. The next time you hear about a few 'hot stocks' to watch or Marty Zweig* says he likes XYZ or ABC Company, please understand that they already have their position built. What do you think... he wants twenty million buyers competing with him as he tries to accumulate shares? NO WAY! Not only that, but he could change his mind tomorrow and you would never know!"

*One footnote:

I pick on Marty Zweig ONLY because he has a very good comedy name! If there was a guy named *"Pickle"* I'd use him.

The audience goes wild over stuff like this! They feel as if someone, for the first time, is telling them the real story...and they're happy as clams. There are hundreds of similar examples of things you can "uncover" to give them a look behind the curtain. I promise you this will make them smile.

Keep in mind, however, that stories like these are not major portions of the presentation, they are short, humorous or poignant inserts designed to spice up a presentation. I wouldn't dwell on them for more than a minute or two at most. In fact they're best delivered almost as asides or throw-aways.

How the "Big Boys" do it

The second way to share this insider's perspective is less dramatic but equally effective. When you explain a basic investment concept such as diversification, include with your explanation a little history of the concept. The migration of ideas and investment practices in our industry seems to progress from large institutional money to small institutional money to large individual money to Mom & Pop. The managers of the General Motors pension plan were doing tactical asset allocation long before it became popular for a $2,000 IRA.

As we on the retail side have become more sophisticated and as technology has enabled us to incorporate these strategies into our portfolios, we're actually doing the same types of analysis and portfolio construction that they were doing at GM 20 years ago.

Knowing that they have access to the techniques of the largest, most successful institutional or private investors makes your audience feel happy. So if you plan to talk about an investment technique or strategy that has its roots in a "higher level" of professional money management, bring that history into the discussion. It will help make a stronger case and elevate you in the eyes of your audience.

Knowledge is important...but what counts is
How you package it

Think back for a second to your college days. Did you ever have a professor who really made a subject come alive? One who dispensed knowledge with excitement and made the subject fun. I had one such professor for Intro to Genetics. (Yes, I was a Biology major.) Talk about a tough subject filled with facts and complex details...all I remember was that I loved going to class. He made every class fun and stimulating. We were learning, we were laughing, we were intrigued and made more curious by every bit of knowledge. Every day was a thrill. It still makes me smile.

There is no doubt that we learned more having fun than we would have if the class had been boring. And believe me, it could have been very boring. Yet he realized that this was a great subject, filled with fascinating discoveries.

It's the same with investing. To most people, ours is an arcane world filled with powerful people all doing things they can't understand with interest rates, and monetary policy and stock prices. They hear about it every day from the media, and they know that everything has some impact on their lives, but they don't understand it at all.

They know they need help. They know they need knowledge. They're desperately seeking someone who can lead them out of confusion and into enlightenment. But at the same time, they can't devote a lot of energy to understand it. After all, they're busy with their own world of business or family.

We think all they want is the information so we cram our seminars full of it — to the point that it squeezes out the fun. They will sit through a "no-fun" seminar because it's what they expect. They know from experience that most investment seminars are as boring as watching ozone deplete, so they will take the information and start glancing at their watch after 5 minutes.

If we make learning about money difficult or boring, they will turn off. They won't turn off to *investing*, because obtaining knowledge in this subject is a critical life-need that remains unfulfilled. They will simply turn off to YOU.

Hey...wake up!

I'm about to make a major philosophical point here.

I believe that truly successful seminar presenters are able to share the valuable investment information they possess in such a way that the audience is captivated and enthralled by the presentation. Those are the catalysts to HAPPINESS and happiness is the key to understanding. The more they're enjoying your seminar...the more value you can give them. This belief proceeds from the premise that the world of money and investing is intensely fascinating and fun once you understand it. Chances are that you feel the same way, or you wouldn't be here today. So why allow your seminars to carry anything less than the full level of enthusiasm for this exciting world. Your emotional attachment to the subject will directly transfer to the audience. They will feel as you feel. The next question is obvious.

Are you having fun yet?
Enjoy yourself

A happy presentation starts with *your* attitude. Is this seminar a fun event for YOU...or are you dragging your butt in after a tough day at the office all sloppy and tired just trying to get it over with?

If they feel your energy and enthusiasm...it will infect them and they will begin to get happy too. To this end I always try to keep a thought in my mind. I remember that these people gave of their own time to come hear ME? Who the Hell am I? Some fat Italian kid from Staten Island with a slightly above average vocabulary and a Series 7? Recalling my humble roots makes me feel thrilled that they showed up. This feeling comes through because I'm genuinely glad to see them and I love talking to people about investing. (The only thing I love more is talking to people about TALKING! Can you tell?)

I'm their ticket to the big game. I'm their connection to the world of finance and investing. It's a role you should cherish. It's richer than any Broadway character.

I'm overemphasizing this aspect of your attitude because most of you have been *under*-emphasizing it for far too long. I've been to hundreds of seminars all across this country and it's clear to me that very few investment professionals recognize the role they're being asked to play.

This business isn't about money...it's about psychology.

This reality is only now starting to spread through the financial planner community. It will hit the wirehouses next but it may *never* make it to portfolio managers.

When you make the decision to do investment seminars, I think you've got to get a little excited. If you're incapable of getting excited or so burdened by your day-to-day responsibilities that you perpetually wear what I call the "fiduciary frown," then why bother getting up in front of an audience. Stick to the telephones. You'll be much better off and your clients will too.

So that's #1 — be happy yourself. Get fired up about everything around you...the risks, the challenges, the rewards, the winning and losing. You're a starting player in the greatest game our society has ever invented. It's a game that powers every aspect of life on this planet. A seminar is your chance to share that feeling with the spectators...people who can only watch from the sidelines while things happen to their money out there on the playing field.

If this role is too much for you and if seminars don't get you excited, why in God's name are you doing them...that's what I want to know.

Make them feel good...
About themselves

People like to feel special and good about themselves and they like people who help them feel good about themselves. That can't possibly be an Earth-shaking revelation.

Let's say you're doing a 7 p.m. seminar. This audience worked a hard day, came home, wolfed down dinner, brushed off the kids, never changed clothes, got back into the car and drove to some hotel to sit for an hour or two to learn about money. In today's society, that ranks up there with Hercules cleaning out the Stygian Stables.

I will often compliment them for taking the time to come and suggest, very directly, that they should feel happy or proud of themselves for making this effort. I don't recommend this at the opening, but maybe half- or two thirds of the way into the talk I'll give them a feel-good pep talk like this:

"Look around. Do you see any of your neighbors here? Anyone from work or your club? Probably not. Folks, YOU are the ones who took the time to come here tonight. I know you're busy and there are a million things you would rather be doing, but you just made a wise investment in your future. This two hours will arm you with some very important knowledge that you need to reach your financial goals. I applaud you and I think you can tell that I'm trying to give you some real value for your time! Let's get back into it."

Now they're sitting there feeling delighted with themselves thinking, *"Hey, I AM a really good person for coming here tonight!"* They're also delighted with you for recognizing their effort.

OK it's time to get to the biggie...
HUMOR!

I was going to make this a separate chapter, but it really does come under HAPPINESS, so we'll do it now.

Humor plays a major role in my seminars (as you may have guessed), but be warned that humor is also the most difficult speaking concept or skill to master and incorporate comfortably into a presentation. Ask any professional actor and they will tell you that comedy is a hundred times harder than drama. The good news is that you can improve very quickly with practice and experience.

The first piece of advice is to just relax and don't try to be funny. It's very hard for people to be humorous when they're thinking *"I've got to be funny now!"* Audiences can feel your stress and they will get tense themselves. So if you're going to use humor, make it natural low-effort.

Why use humor?

• A more enjoyable flow

Humor lubricates the emotional and logical processes of a public presentation better than any other mechanism. It also creates a sense of fun that permeates the entire seminar event and puts people in the right frame of mind to consider a relationship with you.

• Humor keeps their attention

The audience is more likely to stay tuned to the presentation. The human attention span has shrunk dramatically over the past decade. I call it the *"Remote Control Syndrome."* Think back to your last seminar. Did you notice people's minds begin to wander? Did your audience stay focused throughout your presentation? Here you are, deep into your thorough analysis of second-level derivatives and their use in foreign stock option short-against-the-box inverse cross-hedging. The next sound you hear will be one gigantic **CLICK** as they simultaneously switch channels to their own mental version of the Home Shopping Network.

Humor keeps them interested. It keeps them awake and excited. It nurtures a sense of the unexpected making them feel that no matter how serious or technical you may get, or how their attention may temporarily wander — there is something stimulating and fun coming just around the corner.

• Easier to digest complex subjects with humor

Humor can help you navigate through the seminar and make the move from one sub-topic to another. It gives the audience a chance to catch their breath and relax their minds for a moment. This greatly aids the digestion process. Remember, you're feeding them lots of important information about a very critical subject. You've got to insert several mental rest periods into your presentation...like sherbet breaks between courses in a meal. These are likely to fall at the natural transitions in your seminar outline. A little levity can spice up the transition phase and prepare them mentally for the next concept.

- ### Remember with a smile

Humor is one of the best memory aids known. If you've got something you absolutely want them to remember, maybe a statistic or a fundamental investment concept — tie it to a humorous story, a funny anagram or even a funny physical gesture. Get them to laugh and smile and they are ten times more likely to recall whatever it is you want them to remember.

Just think about this book for example. I want you to remember the emotional hot-buttons and mind states of a seminar audience. I could have simply listed them in alphabetical order. But somehow, linking them up with the acronym LURCH FACE had a certain appeal. You may forget some of the words attached to these letters, but the chances are that you will always see the face of Lurch from The Addams Family and you'll remember *something*.

- ### Humor helps you in nearly every speaking situation

Humor is like the Swiss Army knife of public speaking. From time to time in your career you may find yourself in different presentation situations that might be awkward or uncomfortable. Maybe you've got a hostile room. Maybe you're stuck in a tough Q&A session. Maybe the slide projector broke or the microphone blew up in your hand. Being able to use appropriate humor at the right time can save the life of your presentation.

In the beginning, you're like a small Swiss Army knife — the one with a small blade and a nail file. As you get more adept at using humor you become more flexible and resilient as a presenter. No situation will unnerve you. It's like having one of those really BIG knives...you know the ones with the chain saw and micro-chip lithography machines.

- ### One more reason...

I've given you the tangible reasons for developing your skills with humor. There's also an intangible reason — a sense of humor, in my experience, is a sign of intelligence, maturity, sophistication and professionalism. People who are at the top of their profession are usually very comfortable with relaxed humor. The best public speakers *certainly* are. This is a big picture image thing, but I think

I'm right about this. You be the judge. Whatever the case, it can't hurt to develop an understanding of humor and its use in a presentation.

Some of you may be thinking...

"Hey...wait just a minute here! I'm a financial professional with a lot of important information about interest rates and stock market analysis and economic predictions. These people came to hear everything I know about investments. I've been in this business twenty years and by God when they leave here they're going to know how smart I am. I don't have time for humor!"

All I can say is that the goal of a public seminar is NOT to show the world what you know...it's to market and position yourself as someone they want to do business with. You go a very long way toward starting or enhancing this relationship by making your seminars an enjoyable, enlightening and entertaining experience. Humor plays a major role in this process.

Humor is NOT comedy

When we say "humor" we're not talking about stand-up comedy. That's way too far over the line. Always remember that you are an investment professional. If I was a potential client, I'd likely be fearful of someone who was too outlandish or too funny. In any public presentation, there is an appropriate use of humor. The trick is to find the level and mixture that's right for you and your audience, and then to control the timing and distribution of humor to perfectly blend the entertainment with the information so that you enhance the overall impact of your presentation.

Keep It relaxed & comfortable

Comfortable is important. The object here is not to make people feel threatened by your use of humor. Uncomfortable humor may be derisive, insulting, confrontational, excessively sarcastic or neurotic. You've seen many comics use various types of uncomfortable humor with good success...in comedy environments. It won't work in an investment seminar. So Howard Stern is out.

In an investment seminar, I think humor should be used to uplift and positively stimulate the audience, assuming that's the emotional essence of the message you're delivering. Unless you're very skilled, your use of humor should compliment and coincide with the main tone of your presentation. For advanced speakers, the controlled use of contra-stylistic humor can be a very powerful technique. For example, this is where you might take a very serious message and deliver it in a light, comical fashion. Or vice versa with a trivial point covered in a somber and stoic style. But it's difficult to describe let alone master, so don't worry about it for now.

Humor is personal

What to you may seem like a real howl may be ho-hum or bad taste to someone else. Rule #1 in using humor in a public presentation is NEVER OFFEND ANYONE. The quickest way to lose an entire room is to be offensive or to use inappropriate humor. Even people who think you're hysterical will never dare laugh for fear of creating collateral offense.

If you have something funny to say but you think there's the slightest chance someone might be offended — **DON'T SAY IT!** These days, the politically correct pendulum has a razor-edge. Inappropriate or off-color humor in a public presentation could cost you your job! So use good judgment. Carelessly spoken, a word becomes a weapon that can never be withdrawn and could easily turn on its user. I've seen it happen countless times with devastating effect.

The Basics of Humor

Several formats

Humor comes in several different formats: the joke, the story, the one-liner, the quip and the sight gag, (an expression, mannerism or other physical situation). Each of these has a fairly specific formula and may be used to greater or lesser effect depending on the circumstances.

Also, don't even worry about being spontaneously humorous. Sure, everyone can be witty or hysterical at times and often it just leaps out with little forethought. But you can't do it consistently, under pressure and with positive emotional impact...so don't try.

Humor, even in professional circles, is rarely ad lib. The only comic performers in Hollywood or on TV who are allowed to routinely go off-script are Robin Williams, Billy Crystal, Bill Cosby, Whoopie Goldberg and Jim Carey. That's five in a world of six billion people. Being the office jokester doesn't get you into this club. The majority of the humor we mere mortals use in a public seminar should be carefully planned and practiced. That's OK because good planning and rehearsal can make it seem as though everything is spontaneous, and the audience will THINK you're naturally funny.

What about jokes?

You've probably seen those books of Public Speaking Jokes. Professionals, toastmasters and lecture-circuit types have been using them for decades with great results. For the novice or intermediate-level seminar presenter, these little quips and short humorous anecdotes can be an effective weapon — BUT they require practice so that they come out in a natural style. There's nothing worse than an inexperienced speaker or someone who is not naturally funny, desperately trying to BE funny with a memorized joke. This is one of life's uniquely uncomfortable moments.

For me, written jokes are never spontaneous enough. I prefer to develop my own quips and anecdotes tailor-made for the audience at the time. This is a skill that requires the ability to listen and observe an audience.

Should you feel the urge to tell an actual joke, try to make it as natural as possible. Make the transition from discussion to joke as seamless as you can. A simple two-beat pause will work well as the entry to a joke. You've seen speakers who telegraph a joke. It's like shouting *"OK here's a joke now!"* It doesn't work. Also, if the joke is the only fun and humorous thing you're going to say all night...don't use it. It will stand out like a sore thumb and draw attention to the fact that you are uncomfortable with humor.

Self-effacing humor

The easiest way to get others smiling is to smile and laugh at yourself. Remember, you're having fun so go ahead and show it. Laughing at or making mild fun of yourself is called self-effacing humor. It's a great tool which can be used as part of a very effective and relaxing opening.

"Before we get started, I'm required by the SEC to inform you that I am Sicilian and I live on Staten Island." (These are two traits of major Mafia bosses. This opening works well back East...others may not get the joke.)

"I don't say that to scare anyone. But you need to know because sometimes I get a little excited up here. I really

love talking about (SEMINAR TOPIC) and I can get a little emotional. So if I start to get too enthusiastic, throw a roll at me and I'll calm down. By the way, the people in the front row each get an extra cookie as a reward. Sitting so close to me can be hazardous."

Obviously, you can't use that specific opening, but why not build something similar about yourself?

I'm also someone who very obviously enjoys eating. I may say, *"Folks, you'll have to pardon me if I lose my concentration tonight. On the way in I caught a glimpse of the cheese cake in the back and my mind may wander."*

I may return to that joke later in the night, especially if I actually should lose my train of thought.

"I'm sorry, it's that cheese cake again!"

Try not to overdo the self-effacing humor. There is a line beyond which you begin to lose respect and credibility. I will rarely make a joke about my investment expertise or industry knowledge. Most of my self-effacing quips are physical or personal, something that lets them laugh at my human side...NOT my professional side.

Funny headlines

One of the best at this technique is Mark Freeman from American Funds. Audiences love it every time. He begins his seminar by saying something like...

"This is a confusing time to be an investor. No wonder people have trouble making decisions. Look at the headlines in the newspapers."

And then he begins to pull out headline clips from major papers...all taken on the same day. Naturally, these are carefully culled to illustrate a point...that the media has no idea what they're doing and the financial advice they give investors is contradictory to the point of being hysterical.

I love to add a headline from some tabloid...

"Elvis Spotted Piloting Alien Saucer"

It sort of puts a capper on the theme.

Cartoons

If you're using any visual aids like slides, overheads or computer graphics, these can add a lot of laughs without requiring you to be too funny yourself. You can find these in any number of places. I subscribe to the New Yorker Magazine just to cut out the cartoons. Sometimes, you might find a cartoon with a really funny picture that has nothing to do with your subject. Use it anyway and suggest your own caption. You can really have fun with this.

Make fun of them

It is also OK to poke a little fun at the audience. You want to wait until you've built up some rapport before roasting them, but they like to laugh at themselves too. You don't want to slip into Comedy Club mode, but laughter makes the event more fun.

A good example of this mild jesting can be seen in the story of inflation we told earlier. If the mood strikes me and I think the audience can handle it, I will pick members of the audience to play the various roles. Someone becomes Lyndon Johnson and Jimmy Hoffa and Ronald Reagan.

"At one end of the table is President Lyndon Johnson. At the other end of the table is a man who is today the most famous corpse in America...Jimmy Hoffa."

Whoever you pick to play Hoffa will get a laugh. You can have some fun with this if you like...

"He looks a little like Jimmy...not today of course."

There are many ways to poke mild fun at the audience, this is only one. You should find the humor in your talk and build specific segments into the presentation as possible "fun spots." If you sense the crowd is with you, go ahead and use them.

Keep it simple

Humor works best in small doses applied sparingly throughout your presentation. Avoid long, drawn out stories or jokes or a continuous barrage of comedy. The main reason you're there is to deliver an important message about money and investing. The humor, as important as it is, must take a back seat.

I know an excellent public speaker who is funny, witty and very interesting. But just when the audience starts to get caught up in his presentation he transforms as if possessed by some comedy demon and he starts going wild. In acting parlance, he starts *"chewing up the scenery."*

He goes into these long, ridiculous jokes with absurd foreign accents and facial mannerisms and obscure punch lines which leave the audience sitting there wondering, *"Can he possibly think he's being funny?"* This costs him significant credibility.

He's missed the point of humor. He force-feeds you a heavy side dish of unnatural humor instead of using a light dash to spice up his main presentation.

Tailor it to the event

Not all presentation formats are the same and you've got to structure your use of humor around the needs of the audience. The after-dinner speaker, for example, needs a whole different set of humorous inserts than the keynote speaker at a symposium.

If this is your event, the people are coming specifically to see you. Here, the use of humor can be more standardized as part of your normal presentation. But let's say you're the guest speaker at the local Lions Club or the Kiwanis or some other organization. Now you may need to inject more humor into your talk. Often, the program chairperson can give you some insights as to the group's expectations. Do they want a serious talk or are they looking forward to a very entertaining session? I will talk more about group presentations in a later chapter. They are a world all their own.

Opening with humor

The beginning of your presentation is a great time to use some light humor because it relaxes the audience and eases them into the event. The type of humor you use as an opener can vary widely giving you a broad selection from which to choose. For example, you might use a series of humorous quotations, a brief story or a humorous commentary about a headline in the local paper that relates to your topic or to the audience.

The humorous opening has the added benefit of being expected. Most audiences are comfortable with this pattern so using it makes them feel at home.

Risks of a funny opening

There are two main risks to opening with humor. First, you might blow the delivery. This could trip you up right at the beginning of your presentation forcing you to regroup and lose a little early momentum.

The image of an amateur speaker stumbling through an opening with a planned joke has become such a cliche that you should avoid it — with one exception — where you have so fully mastered the delivery that you can actually top the cliche. Done well, a humorous opening makes a strong statement about your confidence as a speaker. But given today's tougher audiences, the risk is too great and the reward is too small for the average speaker.

Second, you might severely misread the audience's personality and tolerance for humor. An audience that you think would be anxious for a few laughs might have undergone a transformation or changed moods with no warning.

I saw one of the most hysterical examples of this on the sitcom Frazier when he was asked to be the guest speaker at a fancy banquet dinner. Unknown to him, the Bishop, who was to deliver the meeting's invocation, was lost at sea in a freak boating accident a few hours before the dinner. This horrible fact was announced to the audience while Frazier was out of the room. I won't recount the dialogue but you can imagine the negative impact of his sarcastic opening remarks as he laughingly roasted the Bishop for not showing up.

The opening segment of a seminar is a dangerous moment for you AND the audience. They don't know what to expect any more than you do. After you get to know each other for a few minutes, the use of humor is much less risky.

Don't assume that because you know one or two people in the room and they are real cards or cut-ups who love a good joke that the rest of the audience will appreciate bawdy or cutting edge humor. Remember the group dynamic. People tend to react much more conservatively in groups than they would as individuals. Your friends could leave you twisting in the wind after a blown opener.

If you absolutely insist on opening with a canned joke...try this. First, practice the joke with all the timing and delivery nuances until you have it down cold. Do it in front of a mirror or with a video camera. Then try it on a group of friends. Practice until you can deliver it with total confidence. Commit to yourself that you will never fumble the opening kick-off.

Then...work on the drama of the moment. Remember that the opening few moments of your seminar are primarily a visual process. The audience hasn't gotten used to the sound of your voice yet, so they're mostly assimilating you through their eyes right now. To make them focus on your words, stand still and slow your hand movements while delivering the joke.

Often, I will begin my opening in a very serious tone. I will slowly and deliberately build into what looks like a serious opening. I want to catch them by surprise with the punch line. Never "telegraph the joke." Far better to keep them guessing right up until the end. The result of this style is often quite exciting and sets a vibrant tone for the rest of the event.

It is not necessary that you drop them to the ground in spasms with your opening joke. Mild laughter is plenty. At this point in the opening, they still don't know you or what to expect. You're not going for the big guffaw. Your goal is simple. You want to leave them thinking, *"Here's a guy who knows how to be funny in an intelligent way. This is going to be a great presentation."*

Here's a good, multi-purpose opener that can be tailored to nearly any group. I don't know who first told this but I've used it for years with good effect. Remember, delivery is crucial. This looks like it's too tedious, but it *tells* much better than it *reads*.

Albert Einstein was on a plane from New York to San Francisco. He turned to the man next to him and asked, *"Pardon me Sir, may I ask, What's your IQ?"*

The man said *"I have an IQ of 145."* Einstein was thrilled. *"145...that's wonderful. I'd love to discuss literature, music and philosophy with you. This certainly is going to be an interesting trip."*

He then turned to the woman on the other side and asked, *"Madam, may I ask, what's your IQ?"* She replied, *"I have an IQ of 153."* *"153...that's simply remarkable,"* Einstein cried! *"We can discuss physics, astronomy and mathematics. This is going to be fun."*

He then turned to a fellow sitting across the aisle and asked *"Sir, please may I ask what's your IQ?"* The man said proudly *"I have an IQ of 43."* Einstein paused... *"A forty three IQ, huh? (PAUSE) How'd the market close?"*

A little old, but it still works.

Finally...humor must fit
Your style

We've covered only the tip of the humor iceberg. Ultimately, what matters is your own personal style. Nearly every one of us is funny in a different way and what works well for someone like me may be disastrous for you.

In general, when all else fails, always remember that there is something funny and mildly laughable in everything around us. Simple reflection, more than concentrated effort to be funny, is often all you need to evoke happiness in an audience. I'm certain you're more than capable of finding humor in life or in a given situation. Let that natural side of you show through.

Let your use of humor be a reflection of your character. It is one of the most personal things you can share with an audience. Assuming you're not off the deep end, they will respond enthusiastically to almost any use of positive humor. You will not come across as forced or as trying too hard. Chances are even a small effort will not go unrewarded and you will have succeeded in the larger goal of making an audience happy.

CHAPTER 9

FEAR

"To conquer fear is the beginning of wisdom."
Bertrand Russell

FEAR AND GREED ARE THE GREAT MOTIVATORS. We all learned that lesson on the first day of Investment Sales 101. Today, however, fear is a much bigger motivator than greed. This may depend on your client base, but overall, serious investors are much more afraid of losing money or taking too much risk than they are hungry to make a "killing."

That makes fear the single most powerful emotional tool for moving a crowd to action. Two potential problems with this: First, if all you do is scare them, they won't like you. You've violated our first emotional rule. Clients want to see you as their white knight...a savior, not a demon. Second, too much fear and you don't motivate anyone. Instead, you paralyze them into inaction.

Despite these risks, you must learn how to make an audience feel fear in a seminar. You will find it an invaluable component of nearly every presentation. Used well, it will not only make your seminars more informative and entertaining but it will lead to results!

Did he say "entertaining?" You bet. Fear is fun when used properly. People like to be scared. Why do we go to see horror movies or read scary books? Fear in a seminar is part of the entertainment process just like humor. In fact, the juxtaposition of fear and humor are a deadly one-two punch we'll discuss in a second.

What's the objective...
Your goal for fear

During the body of your presentation, your goal should be to generate enough fear to make everyone recognize the need for action and change, but not *too* much so that they walk out shaking their heads in panic and despair.

They've got to understand that if they keep doing what they're doing, they will end up with a result they don't want. That can be any one of a hundred things depending on the content of your presentation. The fear should be tailored to the main message.

In that sense, fear is like a mythical dragon. In a seminar, you first want to create the dragon — make it as frightful and dangerous as you think they can stand...and then, with your skill and expertise, slay this dragon right in front of them. The good news is that you get to create your own dragon because it's your seminar and you're in control of the emotional process.

Hey, wait a minute
Is fear fair?

Good question. Let's clear up the ethics of fear as a tool right now!

Fear exists in everyone's mind and heart...especially when it comes to money! You're not really creating fear, you're simply tapping into it; perhaps redefining it and focusing it. Depending on the audience, you will be able to access many different types of fear — fear of losing money, fear of missed opportunity, fear of poverty, fear of looking foolish, fear of success and wealth, just to name a few. No subject gives you greater entree to a person's set of fears than money with the possible exception of sex...and both are very closely related subjects.

By itself, fear is neither good nor bad. Our purpose in a seminar is to use a controlled exposure to fear to get people thinking and acting in their own best interests. This is a valuable service and there is nothing unethical or wrong about it.

If, on the other hand, you use fear to mislead and exploit people, you should be taken out and shot. There is no place for you in our business.

The wonder of fear in a public seminar is that it clarifies the emotional message. By properly accessing an audience's fears about money you can move them toward positive behaviors. To use fear in a presentation you must know your audience, be able to anticipate and read their emotional reactions and be able to tailor your message based on the feedback you get from them.

It helps here to know a little about Neuro-Linguistic Programming (NLP). This is a skill set that will enable you to notice the changes that take place in your audience when you start talking the fears they have. Their body language shifts to a defensive posture and their eye movements indicate memory accessing. They're recalling that mental image of fear. NLP works even better one-on-one.

Which one to use?

Two types of fear

There are two broad classes of fear – intellectual fear and emotional fear. They go together and are often present in the same situation. Intellectual fear is the way most people will verbalize what they're feeling to you. Remember, they want you to think they're sophisticated, logical investors. Emotional fear is the actual feeling itself. It's hard to put into words but it's the key to reaching an audience.

For example, an elderly couple may be intellectually afraid of "out-living their portfolio income." That's way too logical but that's what most financial advisors talk about. Emotionally, what scares them is the thought of moving in with their children or of being unable to afford hospital care in the case of serious illness, or of waiting by the door for the mailman to arrive with the Social Security check so they can buy groceries.

These are the mental pictures that give them goose bumps and will prompt them to action, not the dry dollars and percentages of an actuarial analysis.

An investor trying to grow his asset base may be coaxed into overly risky investments because he intellectually fears a below average rate of return. Emotionally, he fears looking stupid in the eyes of his colleagues who may have taunted him with stories of exaggerated returns and market prowess. He doesn't want to be seen as too conservative...not a "player" or missing out on a "sure thing."

The emotional pictures everyone carries within them are so powerful that they become an unconscious screening mechanism which automatically activates at the mention of the word "investing." As soon as you bring up the subject, they will pass all data through their fear screen and discard much of what doesn't match their emotional concerns.

Simply put, if you ignore their fears and fail to address their emotional issues about money — they will not buy your message or you. Your goal is to concentrate your emotional message so that you reach a broad band of fears and by doing so, demonstrate that you understand their basic concerns and are prepared to address them.

What's the best way to...
Scare them?

And scare them you must, but remember we said that fear can paralyze. What good is it to scare them into a catatonic state too afraid to even set an appointment with you?

On occasion, I will turn into one of those "fire & brimstone" speakers who can deliver fear straight up with both barrels. More often, however, I will soften the fear through the use of stories, quotes and anecdotes. But more than anything, I find it best to mix fear with humor. *(In fact, I find it best to mix nearly everything with a little humor.)*

There's a simple reason for this and you can see it illustrated on the adjacent chart. When you deliver fear too forcefully, you will quickly move up the motivation curve until you reach a point of maximum motivation. Pass that point, and their motivation begins to drop slowly until you reach VAPOR LOCK at which point it drops like a rock. You've sacred them too much and they've shut down to further emotional input.

When you mix fear with humor, look at what happens. Their motivation curve rises more slowly, but stays at a higher peak much longer. When it drops it falls more slowly and not nearly as far. You get to deliver a higher dosage of fear and, even in a worst case scenario, you won't paralyze them.

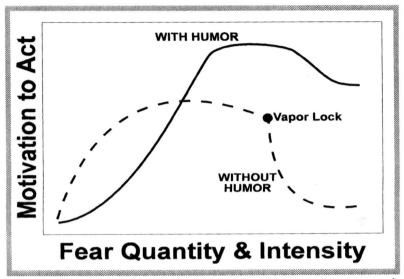

Fear Quantity & Intensity

In some ways the use of fear becomes like an amusement park roller coaster. The humor is like the big safety bar — it reassures them that they are not going to fall out of the seat and plummet to their death — so they're more eager to take the dangerous yet exciting ride. Without the safety bar, virtually no one could stand the risk. They will let you scare them more if they know they're safe.

Also, to carry this analogy further, every roller coaster ride has a few flat sections. How long could you last if you stayed in a sixty degree banking nose dive for the whole ride...not too long. In your seminar, you can use humor and varied delivery techniques to break the fear up into more comfortable dosages. The net result is much better message retention, higher overall motivation and substantially greater enjoyment.

Let me give you a simple example of this fear with humor mixture. Here's a scene I call *"The Dreaded Phone Call."*

"Folks, my parents are retired now and getting old. How many of you have parents who are sixty five or older. (PAUSE) Then you know what I'm going through."

"Their concerns about money are very real and very painful, just like millions of Americans today who are in or getting close to retirement. What they fear, what

*keeps them awake at night is the 'Dreaded Phone Call.'
It goes something like this . . . "*

Slow your pace and lower your voice. Watch how the room gets quiet with everyone focusing on you. They're getting into the emotions of the story.

"Son, remember how your Dad and I helped you with college. And we were there for you whenever you needed some money — your first car, your house. Well, we're getting old now and honestly, we just can't make it on our own anymore. (PAUSE) We were kind of hoping you and Rebecca had room for us because we may need to move in with you for a while."

You will see a very powerful reaction in the crowd. The fear has reached them on a deep, gut level, but because it's such an emotional fear, you can't let it sit there too long, so now you can break the tension with a little humor.

Still serious . . . very deadpan.

"Now I'm lucky. I'm a financial professional. I'm ready for this phone call. I've prepared. (PAUSE) Every six weeks I change my phone number and my parents will never reach me."

Everyone laughs. The emotional fear torpedo has hit its intended target but you don't want them to drown, so you lift them up with a little humor and then move on.

"Ah, you laugh, but it's a very real fear. Many investors today are scared to death about outliving their income. They actually worry about living too long! Think about that! They're healthy, energetic and ready to enjoy life, but they've run out of money and they have to move in with their kids. What could be more frightening than that...not only for them...but for their children too!"

Now I can transition into my next point of discussion.

You can embellish or dramatize the Dreaded Phone Call story with as much emotion as you can muster. A little crack in the voice or a slightly hoarse, end-of-breath delivery has been known to cause tears to flow!

Fear with humor is easier to swallow and easier to remember. It also lets you increase not only the total dosage of fear but the variety of fears without reaching a saturation point. For example, I may want them to feel the fear of outliving income, taxes going up, about missing a strong growth market and loss of purchasing power all in the same half-hour. If I hit each fear too directly and too hard, they will turn off. With humor, I can compound their emotional state until Part 2 when I lead them away from the precipice and tell them the solutions to their problems.

Tell them a...
Scary story

Stories or anecdotes are a great way to scare them and still keep them safe from too much harm. A good story allows you to illustrate a very frightening scenario and allows the audience to maintain a comfortable emotional distance from the devastation. The CD story I told in an earlier chapter is a good example. Does it get the point across? You bet. But it's not so severe as to cause vapor lock.

Tell them how the "victim" in your scary story felt. This leads them straight to the emotions you want *them* to feel.

Scary stories with happy endings are great too. Particularly if you were the cause of the happiness. Be careful not to overdo this. It could come off as too self-aggrandizing.

The power of the press
Scary quotes & headlines

You want to talk about masters at using fear to motivate...look no further than the popular press. They know that bad news sells and they use it every chance they get. They will help you illustrate any fear-point you could want to make. You should have a file filled with great headlines like:

RETIREMENT AN IMPOSSIBLE DREAM

MARKET POISED FOR A PLUNGE

BONDS NO HAVEN FOR SAFE MONEY

I love these kinds of attention-getters. If you want to have some fun, use a group of three or four real headlines in a row and then hit them with another tabloid headline...

WOMAN GIVES BIRTH TO BAT BOY

Equating or associating the "serious" media with the sensationalist "tabloid" media is a great way to have a little fun and to put the press in its proper position. The public places far too much faith in the media as a source of valid investment advice. Anything you can do to disturb that unhealthy reliance is good.

This headline technique sends them a message to be a little scared but not to take the press too seriously. Times may be tough but you're going to show them a way out.

In addition to headlines, you can find some great quotes or statistics to help you tap into the fear they're feeling. These may need less framing since they're predisposed to believe bad news, so you can use several in a row to generate a good "dramatic build."

This is crazy...
Why Bother with fear?

If you think I'm insane with all this talk of fear, it may be well worth your while to ask your clients and prospects about their fears. What images come to mind when they emotionalize concepts like RISK and REWARD. What kinds of things make them feel happy or scared about their investments?

This is the subject of another book, but too many of us try to sell to prospects on a purely intellectual level. We try to dazzle them with how much we KNOW. We never realize that they live in a world where money and investing is as emotional a concept as love, sex or death.

Think about this — nearly 65% of the investment dollars today are in the name of someone who has a direct personal knowledge of the Depression. If you don't think fear plays a major part in their decision process, think again. That's why you must try to get the fears on the table and shed light on them. In this way, you can direct the fear for positive purposes and get the audience to take constructive action.

And remember, fear is totally in keeping with the 70% entertainment rule. They will love the emotional ride. An audience looks forward to a speaker who can get their juices flowing and are really thrilled when you deliver a message with some emotional impact. As the most powerful emotion, Fear MUST play a leading role in your effort.

CHAPTER 10

ACTION

"Knowledge must come through action; you can have no test which is not fanciful save by trial."
Sophocles

"The great end of life is not knowledge but action."
Thomas Henry Huxley

FOLLOW-UP BEGINS DURING the actual seminar! It starts with a call-to-action that usually comes near or at the end of the event. This segment should outline in very precise terms the next steps the audience must take to achieve whatever goal you identified for them in the beginning of the seminar.

A powerful call-to-action paves the way for the vital post-seminar sales process and can lead directly to new business in the days following the event. A weak action call can leave people confused and unwilling to make a move.

If there is a failure at this point it occurs at two ends of the spectrum — asking too little and asking too much. This is the time to remember that your overall goal of the event is to get people to come in and see you...to set an appointment. You can't expect them to make financial commitments at the seminar.

What you want is for them to take a small baby step in your direction. To do this you must make it very easy and comfortable for them and you've got to give them a reward for doing it.

Use action words

The call-to-action begins with your use of language. Your words should be visual and physical. Get them out of the intellectual and into the sensory reference frames of touch and sight. For example, of the two statements below, which makes you want to move?

1. *"Now is a very opportune time to incorporate a group of globally diversified investments into your portfolio."*

or

2. *"Right now, tonight when you get home...sit down, pull out your investment file. You know, the big brown envelope with stubs from 1986...take a red pen and check off 30% of your total investment portfolio that can be transferred from domestic investments into an overseas stock or bond mutual fund. Start with the worst performing stocks and move down the list until you get to 30%. The first place to go is Europe, then Asia then Latin America. Here's a list of the funds you should consider."*

Clearly #2 has more specificity and more tactile language. I want them to picture themselves sitting down going through their portfolio. I want them to imagine the action in their minds like a golfer creating the image of the perfect approach shot. By making the action come alive for them verbally and breaking it down into small simple movements (*sit down, take a red pen, check off...*), I can get them one step closer to actually DOING something.

No more than
Three steps

You must give them very specific steps to take and keep it simple. Limit your action steps to three. The human mind has trouble absorbing more than three of anything. If you have more than that, try to group them into three broad "action categories." That will allow you to go into more detail within each category, but not too much so that they're confused. By keeping the steps simple, implementation becomes more manageable.

For example, you might have as your three steps:

- Extend maturities on fixed income investments
- Diversify globally with 20-45% of your portfolio

- Focus your domestic portfolio on growth-oriented, mid-cap companies

That's plenty for the average person to digest in one sitting. Of course, you need to carefully disclaim these items because no one idea is perfect for everyone in the audience. That's why they must sit down and talk to you, which leads to the most critical action they can take, and your ultimate goal of the seminar, setting an appointment.

The ultimate action step
"Come in and see me!"

Doing a seminar without setting follow-up appointments is like eating your way through a box of Cracker Jacks and not getting a prize. All you get is popcorn stuck in your teeth and no reward.

Appointments are the reward because they are the only way most people will ever become your client. It's the next logical step for them to take in the process — to sit down and apply the knowledge they've learned during the seminar to their specific investment needs...under the watchful guidance of a trusted professional.

You get appointments by asking for them in a very professional and low-key way. Some would advise you to be more aggressive at this stage in the seminar...to close the sale. But I'm not sure that's correct.

If you've done the kind of seminar we've been talking about in this book; if you've hit the emotional stops along the way and delivered the presentation with enthusiasm, honesty and humor...you will find that the audience is EAGER to meet with you. It's not going to take arm twisting or clever gimmicks to get them in. You will set appointments with 75% of the audience right there at the seminar, which is the best time to do it because they will never be more ready to make the commitment.

All of this is delivered calmly and professionally near the end of the seminar right before the finale. This is the critical "close" of your seminar "sale," and it cannot be a hard sell. You've just spent an hour convincing this audience through your words and delivery that you are a high-quality professional who does business differently and better than others in your market.

To come along now at the end and attempt to force them into setting an appointment or making a decision is counterproductive and could undermine your efforts. Pressure at this stage is unnecessary. All you need to say is something like this:

"Folks, you've got to take all this investment advice with one important grain of salt. Each of you is different (pause) *and what works for you* (point to someone) *may not work for you."* (point to someone else.)

"The most important thing you can do right now is make yourself a promise. Commit to yourself that you are going to turn these ideas into action. Don't let this seminar be an academic exercise. And don't do it alone. There is no reason to travel this path all by yourself. We are here to help you."

"In the back of the room are my assistants. I have cleared my calendar all of next week, and they can get you on the schedule for a personal meeting. Please take advantage of this. Take what you've learned here tonight and apply it to your own personal situation. Many of you may find that you're closer to your goals than you imagined. Some of you will make the needed course adjustments to reach those goals while time is still your ally."

"And let me say this...many of you will decide to work with us and some will not. That's OK. You're still taking very positive action. Whatever final decision you make, you will have armed yourself with the highest quality information and most up-to-date analysis possible. No one can do better than that."

You've done your job in the seminar, you've established enough trust and credibility to eliminate the image of "pushy salesperson." They will recognize this as a genuine attempt to help them and they will respond.

Have your people in the back at tables with your appointment book and a handout that tells people what they need to bring with them on their first meeting with you.

As a fallback position...
A free evaluation

Not everyone will want to set an appointment at the seminar. There is no reason to feel bad about this...it's natural. Some may not have responded to your style, some want to think about your message before they commit and others simply need to get home in a hurry.

Take the pressure off. Your goal with these people is simply to get them to take one small step toward action just to break the inertia. To do this, give them something of value — a special research report, an article on a crucial topic, a copy of your newsletter — something to allow you to make another contact. This gives you another chance to reach them. Very often, once they see that you're someone who follows through with no pressure...they will respond.

As a fallback position, you might want to offer a specific financial planning tool they can use such as an asset allocation review. You would ask them to fill out a questionnaire in return for complete diagnostic of their current portfolio holdings. There are a boatload of these tools you can use including a retirement analysis, a college tuition planner, a credit analysis of their bond portfolio, research reports on their stocks or a report on their mutual fund holdings.

Whatever you decide to use should be simple for them to understand. You might want to pass around completed samples of the questionnaire and the reports you're offering. Have your assistants talk them through the sample report. This will allow you to sell them on the benefits of the report and boost your response rate. All this effort is designed to make the call-to-action a physical process where they are writing things down onto paper. This transfer of thoughts from the left brain to the right brain increases the likelihood that they will actually do something as a result of your talk.

The questionnaires should be multiple choice, check the box-type documents. Avoid asking for long answers or complex data. See the Appendix for a sample.

CHAPTER 11

CHANGE

"Nothing endures but change."
Heraclitus

A SEMINAR IS THE CATALYST that initiates a process of change in a prospect's financial world. This change is a very emotion-filled issue involving lots of psychological baggage, pain and distress that makes it very hard to implement.

If you have ever tried to convince someone to transfer their account to you from a broker or advisor they've known for years, you know how difficult this can be. Suddenly, all the logic and facts in the world are useless. Stress levels rise dramatically and objections leap from hidden corners.

Change is pain for many investors — like dental work. But also like dental work, it's often very necessary and will ultimately lead to much greater financial health going forward.

Start by
Overcoming inertia

"An object at rest tends to remain at rest unless acted upon by an external force."

Issac Newton knew his stuff!

Most people have a high degree of inertia built into their portfolios and their existing financial relationships. This feeling of passivity and reluctance to move may exist despite poor performance, bad service and damaging advice. How many times have you met with a prospect who was crucified by a previous advisor and STILL they refused to make a move? It's true.

Before you can effectively get people to make changes during a seminar, you've got to accept that this is going to be a difficult task. Once you've realized that fact, you need to scale back your own expectations of the amount of change you're going to seek during the seminar process.

All you want to do during the seminar is give them a little shove just to get the body in motion...not to accelerate it to Warp 7. Once they are moving, emotionally, you can increase the speed and alter the course of their motion as desired. It's like pushing a stalled car. You're going to expend a lot of energy to start the car moving, but then, it becomes easier to steer and control the speed with much less effort. Save the steering and speed changes for the follow-up appointments. For now...just get them off their butts!

Work with
Two simple messages

Your goal during the seminar is to get across two emotional messages:

> 1. *Change is normal and good.*

> 2. *Change to you has major benefits.*

There is a third message that's best left for the follow-up meeting. This is where you convince them that changing relationships is not going to cost them lots of money, make them feel foolish or force them to confront their other advisors. This is too much for a seminar, so save it.

Normal and good

We know that the investment world is based on constant change, yet to say this to a roomful of investors is scary. They fear change nearly as much as they fear losing money. The best way to bring up the subject of change in a seminar is to do the opposite — highlight the concepts that remain stable and timeless and to cover change as a casual occurrence within a more consistent big picture. What am I talking about? Here's an example of a discussion on change I've used to make the process feel more comfortable.

> **"Folks, the world of investing consists of several time-tested principles that have never and will never**

change. Principles like diversification, like owning high-quality companies with solid earnings, like investing for the long run rather than a short-term time horizon. Sure, names will change and trends will come and go and every portfolio will need updating and revamping from time to time, but these changes are meaningless in the context of your overall investment strategy. They are minor course corrections on the road to your goals.

"People fear change, and not without good reason, but I think it's more a matter of attitude and perception versus reality."

"Investing is a lot like driving. If you know where you are and where you're going, you don't need to worry about the minute steering corrections, speed changes or taps on the brake. These occur a thousand times a minute, but you handle them with ease because you know they are a natural part of driving. If every pothole caused you to slam on the brakes, turn 180 degrees around and head in the opposite direction...you would never get home."

You can have some fun with this driving analogy.

Change to you has benefits

There has to be some reason for doing business with you otherwise people will not make a move. One way to think of this entire segment is as a

Television commercial.

Here's an outline of a possible commercial on CHANGE that might make them more comfortable. You can insert this right after the Q&A and before the close. If you're a little concerned about the Q&A, you might want to use it beforehand. The goal is to place this segment at the point of maximum emotional momentum. If you've done a great seminar and they're really rocking...don't wait for the Q&A...do it now. If you are very good at the Q&A, save it. A good Q&A session will add to the seminar's momentum and enhance your stature. Learn to feel the audience to judge the timing and intensity of events.

Whatever you do, do not attempt any kind of commercial until AFTER the body of the seminar. The mistake most financial professionals make is that they front load the commercial before they've earned the right to do one at all. I can't tell you how many times have I've seen speakers spend the first ten minutes of the seminar telling the audience how they manage people's money and what they would do for anyone who did business with them. Convincing someone to change advisors is hard enough. Doing it in your introduction is pure stupidity. Then they wonder why seminars don't work.

No one gives a crap about you or your incredible capabilities until you've proven by your performance that you're different, smarter and better. AFTER the seminar...that's when you do the commercial. And after the kind of seminar you're going to be giving now, your commercials will hit with tremendous impact and produce wondrous results.

You should modify this to fit your own style because it's not for everyone.

"Ladies & Gentlemen, there are two reasons I conduct these seminars: one is to educate you. Hopefully, we've worked through some of the confusion you may have felt when you walked in tonight."

"My second goal is to encourage you to come to Blowhard, Boggle and work with me. I suspect that won't surprise you."

"Let me give you two reasons you should consider Blowhard, Boggle. One is an emotional reason and the other is a logical reason. Here's the logical reason first:"

"When you come to Blowhard Boggle _____(fill in the blank)"

What makes you or your firm special? What is your philosophy of investing and WHY is this better than your competition approach? You can spend a minute or two doing a simple commercial that appeals to their logical side.

(PAUSE)

"Now, the emotional reason."

Here's another commercial but this time geared toward the emotional side of investing with you and your firm. What is it that makes people feel happy and secure about working with you? What do you do that's exciting and unique? What gives them greater peace of mind?

"The point is that we do things a bit differently at Blowhard Boggle. Maybe you can tell by some of the things we've discussed tonight, that we take a unique and more personal approach to this business. Over time, my clients have come to truly value that approach, and I think you will too."

The Superbowl

To do this well, think of the Superbowl. You're going to produce two, two-minute commercial spots on you and your company that will air on the Superbowl. You've seen ads like this from all sorts of companies. Some are very powerful. Imagine all the creative talent and effort that goes into making those commercials. Well that's what you've got to do now. You've got to give them a reason to make the move...and neither logic nor emotion alone will do the job. It's a combination effect.

I can think of a million possibilities here, but you're the one who must direct these commercials. They've got to come from your heart and mind or they won't work. People are not going to make a move if they can't feel your sincerity at this critical moment. So keep it as simple as you need to, and be natural.

I'm assuming that you HAVE a few good reasons why people should want to do business with you as opposed to anyone else. If not, stop reading right now and come up with them.

"They know I want their business, so...
Why say anything?"

You're right. They probably do know, and most likely you could still do some effective follow-up without this entire segment on change. But what's the point of doing an extraordinary seminar if you're not in search of extraordinary results? I'm talking about close ratios of 75%, 80% even 90% or better. I'm talking about a calendar full of seminars and each one an SRO event. I'm talking about more business than you can imagine. It's waiting out there, and nobody is going after it. Oh, you may have your hook in the water...along with nine billion other financial advisors. But are you "attacking," or simply waiting for the fish to leap into your boat?

Superiority and **excellence** are what this whole book has been about. If you're happy with average results...keep doing what you've been doing...you'll get them. If you want to blow the doors off your business...try what I've been telling you.

The only way you earn the right to do a powerful commercial at the end of a seminar AND have it take meaningful effect...is to do a *fantastic* seminar.

Conversely...if you DO a fantastic seminar...you MUST do a commercial. If not you've just wasted a Patriot missile to kill a mosquito. You've been excellent in pursuit of mediocrity, or at best, you're not serious about growing your business.

I'm sorry. I get a little carried away sometimes. I just want you to feel the potential out here. It's enormous! You've just busted your butt for an hour giving these people knowledge, solving their problems, sharing your valuable insights...now it's time to remember why you're here.

You asked, *"Why should I say anything?"* If you believe that you can help them make positive changes in their financial lives, then you've got a moral obligation to try. You can't help a single soul until they open an account or write some kind of check. There is nothing unprofessional about "asking for the order." It's all in how you ask.

Your approach at this point in the seminar will get them to recognize that change is beneficial and not nearly as scary as they think. If you're feeling really bold, it's even OK to discuss in greater detail the actual mechanics of opening or transferring an account. What will happen on their first visit to see you? How have you handled others who've made the change?

I've found this section to be the most direct, yet non-threatening way to bring up the most important subject of the seminar — them doing business with you. That's the one change they must make from which all the others follow, because, until they are working with YOU, all of this is merely an academic exercise.

CHAPTER 12

ENERGIZED
EXCITED
ENTHUSIASTIC

"Nothing great was ever achieved without enthusiasm."

Ralph Waldo Emerson

L ONG AFTER THE SEMINAR IS OVER...after they've forgotten all your charts, graphs, facts, statistics, indeed after they've forgotten the entire meaning and message of the seminar — they will remember you and your ability to excite, energize and fill them with enthusiasm.

This is a three-word chapter because all three words convey parts of the meaning I'm trying to get across to you here. The three Es are generated by high-quality content, a meaningful message and the proper blend of the other emotions we've discussed. In my opinion, however, they are mainly a function of something called **DELIVERY**. That's a word I should define because I'm going to use it a lot.

> *Delivery* is the whole presentation of an idea; the actual words you speak; the vocalization including inflection, pitch, pace and tone of your voice; your overall energy level; hand, eye and head gestures; body position and movement...everything.

Everyone has a style of delivery. It's not something you turn on and off, it just exists. The goal is to control the delivery of your thoughts so that you can evoke specific feelings and reactions in the audience.

You've heard the old saying, *"It's not what you say...it's how you say it."* That's delivery. Taking a phrase, a sentence or a word and giving it added meaning by packaging it in a certain style delivery.

You control delivery by understanding the many variables involved in a presentation. For example: You can speak the exact same words and change one variable like **word emphasis** and see how the meaning of the sentence changes. Try it...

Here's a simple test. Try it with a different emphasis each time.
"**YOUR** stocks are dogs."   (Not MY stocks...YOUR stocks!)

"Your **STOCKS** are dogs." (Not your funds...your STOCKS!)

"Your stocks **ARE** dogs." (Not last year...they're dogs NOW!)

"Your stocks are **DOGS**."   (Not winners...LOSERS!)

This seems strange or too basic, but note the different feeling and meaning of each sentence. That's just *one variable* in one simple four-word sentence. Imagine how many variables there are in an entire one-hour seminar. It staggers the mind. Yet that's what delivery is all about.

Curtain up...

Light the lights!

As you may have guessed, I've been a stage actor for many years. Once, while in college, I was offered a role in a Broadway show by the famous producer, Joseph Papp. I turned it down out of sheer ignorance and Mr. Papp was so stunned by the stupidity of my decision he was almost speechless...except for one thing he said that stuck with me all these years. He said, *"You're smart kid. The only actors who make any money in New York are the stockbrokers."* Pretty ironic, no?

Doing a seminar is so much like acting that it's scary. In fact, it's very much like a one-person play for which you are writer, director and star. The one difference I can think of is that in a seminar, you're trying to impart real knowledge — stuff that's going to help people retire, educate their kids and live a happier life. In that respect, the *content* of your seminar is more important than a Neil Simon comedy, but the *delivery* techniques are nearly identical.

If seminars are going to be a big part of your career, I would strongly recommend that you consider taking a course in drama at a local college, studying with a drama coach or at the very least, reading a book about acting technique. You need to learn how to transmit emotion with your body and voice — a skill that will prove valuable over the phone as well. This may sound crazy to you, but just think of the time and money you may have spent on golf or tennis lessons. Isn't your career worth the same effort?

Two acting elements have a tremendous impact on the energy and enthusiasm levels you transmit: Vocal variety and physical movement.

It starts with...
The voice

Your voice is like your own personal information superhighway. It functions mainly as a transmitter of outgoing data. Throughout your entire life, the spoken word is the means by which you convey the majority of the information you want people to know. Yet as important as the voice is to your everyday existence — how many of you know anything about how it works or how to make it more effective?

I know that some of you are thinking: *"Hey, my voice is my voice...there's nothing I can do about it."* Or even better: *"The quality of my ideas is what counts...not how I sound!"*

Wrong on both counts, Sparky! There are many things you can do to improve the quality of your voice. In computer jargon this is called "bandwidth." The greater the bandwidth, the more information a data line can carry. By improving the quality and expressiveness of your voice you can convey more information more accurately and with greater impact.

As for the quality of your ideas...if they are so valuable (and I have no reason to doubt this) why are you transmitting them over inferior equipment? It's like broadcasting Placido Domingo with two cans and a string! If you really have something valuable to say...then say it with maximum clarity, fidelity and accuracy. Whether you are doing seminars, talking over the phone or in a one-on-one meeting, improving the vocal delivery of ideas will enhance the receptivity of your message tenfold.

This isn't as hard as it seems. Don't worry. Even a slight improvement will be very noticeable and simply using one or two vocal variation techniques will greatly enhance your presentation.

Vocal exercises

Your voice is like a muscle...just like a bicep or a quad. It's smaller and more complex, capable of great subtlety and power, but it needs to be warmed up, stretched and worked out just like any other muscle in your body if you expect it to perform when called upon.

Unfortunately, any description I can give you about vocal exercises would be weak compared to one hour with a voice coach. There is a pretty good audio-tape program called *The Executive Voice Trainer* published by Dove Audio, 8955 Beverly Boulevard, West Hollywood, CA 90048. Much of this program is geared toward diction and enunciation which are very useful. Tape 4 covers vocal exercises. It will help you with breathing, vocal support, range extension and resonance.

Hum a little tune

The simplest thing you can do immediately is to warm up your voice with humming. Here is an effective exercise you can do just about anywhere, in the car, at your desk or in the shower.

Start with a tone. You know the song "Do Re Me" from The Sound of Music. Just start with "Do," keep your lips closed but your jaw relaxed and the teeth apart. Do not take a deep breath, but rather breathe naturally and comfortably. Simply hold this tone for as long as your breath lasts. This should be somewhere between 5 and 12 seconds. Don't strain or push for volume...just let the air from your lungs flow freely through your vocal cords.

Now move one notch up the scale to "Re" and do it again. Work your way up until you begin to feel uncomfortable...then stop. Don't try to overreach your range at this point. Now work your way back down the scale to the original "Do" tone. At this point, begin to work down the scale to that point of slight discomfort and stop.

*Feeling OK? Now try this. Start with a middle-range
"Do" and work up the scale with one breath. Go
slowly, one beat every second.*

"Do — Re — Me — Fa — So — La — Te — Do"

*Now go down. Remember, you're not actually saying
the words...you're humming the tones. Now move
your starting tone up just a little bit so that your next
"Do" sounds like "Re" did just a minute ago. Work up
the scale again until you feel that slight strain...then
go back down. Don't strain!*

Now work down the scale from the middle "Do" note.

Great! You've just taken a major step toward improving your
voice. Do this for five minutes a day every day for two weeks and
you will see a dramatic difference in how you sound.

"Do" to "Do" up or down the scale is one octave. Most
professional singers have a range of two to three octaves. Mariah
Carey has *five*! That's a lot of range. (So did that woman who sang
"Loving You" back in the 70's. I can't recall her name but she had
a top range that only *dogs* could hear.) You don't need anything like
that. However, most people giving financial seminars have a two
NOTE range...like Barry White disco music...every sound comes out
the same. Ideally, you should work to develop a supported and
sustainable range of two octaves. That will give you plenty of room
to express any emotion that might cross your path. You'll kill them
with "Happy Birthday."

But since you're not doing a musical concert, it's more important
that you work on vocal support. Support of the voice comes from
your mid-body muscle groups. With proper support you will be able
to project your voice clearly without straining. Support work begins
with breathing, posture, placement of the voice within its natural
strength range, resonance within the body cavities and sustainability
of tone.

In simple terms, you will be able to speak more audibly without
running out of air or sound for longer periods of time. This can be a
lifesaver when the microphone breaks and the residents of Shady Rest
Retirement Home & Hearing Aid Testing Lab are sitting there
waiting for your words of wisdom.

The best advice I can give you is to seek professional training. Find a good voice teacher or use the tapes. Four to six hours of training at $25 to $50 per hour will teach you all you need to know about your voice. Continued practice will give you the power and control you need to be a very effective and exciting speaker.

Vocal variety

I would estimate that the sound of your voice represents up to 60% of the total message you're trying to deliver in a seminar. The actual words you say are roughly 20% and your body/eye movements are the other 20%.

Thereisnothingworsethanaspeakerwhodroansonandoninonen everendingsentencewithoutvaryingthetone,pitchorenergyinhisvoice.

Wow, I'm hypnotized. The most timely and exciting topic can be rendered totally impotent by a monotone drone. To create some excitement in the presentation, you must learn how to use your voice and properly vary the four basic vocal elements:

- **Pitch** (high or treble / low or bass)
- **Pace or speed** (fast / moderate / slow)
- **Inflection** (excited through calm)
- **Volume** (shout through whisper)

Words, by themselves will not move people to action. In fact, the words may never make it from their ears to their minds. It is the combination of these mechanical variables that empower the actual words and give them life. It is your delivery that causes them to pay attention, to focus on what you're saying, to listen critically and intelligently and ultimately say, *"Hey this guy really knows what he's talking about. Let's invest with him!"*

The key to vocal variety is to be natural and comfortable. Too much tinkering and overdone variation can be annoying to an audience and make you sound "affected," as if you're purposely trying to manipulate the delivery.

No standard formula

There is no standard vocal formula for creating emotion. Some speakers generate excitement, for example, by getting louder and faster. Others go slower and softer. It all depends on your style. The key is practice. You've got to find what works best for you and it's better to test out the various delivery styles in front of a video camera than to try it cold in a seminar.

During your rehearsal period, tape yourself delivering the seminar's opening segment with various delivery styles. Try an energetic, fast pace. Then try a slower, more deliberate style. Then mix all the variables and see what effect this has on the meaning of the words. You might be amazed to learn that a few minor changes in delivery can double the impact of your opening.

I know an excellent speaker who rehearses the entire presentation from start to finish out loud several times. She practices until the words and phrasings sound completely natural. When speaking without this practice, or presenting extemporaneously, she is terrible – very stilted, confused and hard to understand. But give her time to prepare and she'll knock your socks off!

In an ideal world, you would rehearse the entire seminar. But you don't have time, so at least rehearse the critical passages in the program. This can help with a new seminar as well as one that you've given hundreds of times. Often, we get into vocal ruts that we're not aware of. Taping is critical. I can't tell you how many times I've listened to myself on tape and said *"Geez...I was way too strong here or too weak here."* or *"There's a better way to say this."* or *"I hope nobody heard that!"*

Natural...not lazy

A presentation to a roomful of people should feel as natural as a one-on-one conversation. But if you tried to conduct a seminar with the same level of vocal energy and gentle mannerisms as you use in a normal conversation...no one would be able to hear or see you.

To give the audience the feeling of intimacy that accompanies a private conversation, you've got to boost the intensity and sharpness of every delivery mechanism from physical gestures to your voice.

Use a mike

One way to increase your emotional effectiveness and control in a seminar is to use a microphone. A lavaliere mike is attached to your jacket and requires no hands to use. Your voice is amplified and you can gesture and move normally. The drawback to a "lav" is that you can't control the volume. Every sound is amplified the same way, so if your voice ranges from soft to very loud, you could get annoying drop-off or harsh feedback.

A hand-held mike is different. It can be a much more exciting tool for vocal variation and you will often see the most emotional speakers use one. For example, when you want to get big and bold, move the microphone away from your mouth and allow your volume to build naturally. When you want to bring the audience in close emotionally, turn down the volume, bring the mike in close and whisper.

A microphone can help you create that private feeling of an intimate conversation and still be heard in the back of the room. This can lead to some exciting results.

Build it in on purpose

Construct your presentation around your basic vocal style and make it more exciting by designing vocal variety into the talk. Design specific modules or segments that allow you to get excited. Create phrases that must be said slowly and deliberately with a soft voice. Create others that require a rising tone or a "vocal build."

In the same way that professional speech-writers develop a presentation that delivers emotions in just the right dose at the right time — a well-written seminar allows you to overlay stylistic elements on top of your basic delivery to project the perfect blend of data and emotion.

Insert a few
Dramatic techniques

In addition to the sound of your voice there are specific speaking techniques or tricks you can use to make your presentation more appealing to the ear and richer in emotional content. One of these is...

The Drip

It's like Chinese water torture only good for you. Think about it...one drop on your forehead is meaningless. You might not even feel it. Three straight days of dripping on your forehead will drive you insane.

We don't want to go that far, but the principle is similar. There are segments of your seminar that must be repeated for the message to sink in and have the impact you desire. If you want someone to remember something, tell them three times. If you want them to take action, tell them five times.

You can often use the "instant replay" where you say something, pause and say it again verbatim.

"Folks, fewer than 3% of 65-year-old retirees are financially self sufficient. LET ME REPEAT THAT.. Fewer than 3% of 65 year-old retirees are financially self sufficient."

Then repeat it again using more descriptive language.

"Of the 35 people in the room right now only one one of you will have enough money to maintain your lifestyle when you reach retirement age."

Now put it aside for a few minutes but be ready to come back to it later in the seminar and repeat it again.

"Why is growth important? Well, remember we said earlier that only 3% of retirees will be financially self-sufficient, so you've got to build your asset base and the only way to do that is with growth-oriented investments."

Without knowing why, many people will leave your seminar with that "three percent" statistic floating around in their heads. It will leave an impact.

Parallels

Used as a major tool of political speakers, the parallel (or balance in speaking terms) has a strong emotional effect. A parallel, like many speaking techniques, is usually a statement made in a triad, that is three parts. It has a very distinct delivery and it works because of some innate genetic affinity for things that come in three's, *(which is why good jokes build on triad form)*. Here's an example:

"Stocks are the best source of growth in the 90's."

"Stocks are the best source of rising income."

(PAUSE)
"Stocks are the best way to meet your financial goals!"

The words *"Stocks are the best"* form the base of the triad. Each statement is delivered with slightly different emphasis on the variable portion, in this case "growth, income and goals."

Try it again, only with a slight switch in structure.

"Keeping your money in the bank will not allow you to retire."

"Investing in bonds will not allow you to retire."

"Buying real estate will not allow you to retire."

"The only investment that will allow you to retire...is stocks!"

You can use this form several times in your presentation with great effect. It gets the message across nicely and adds a professional touch. By the way...I've never seen a seminar *written* like this. You won't get this from the company's slide show.

Figures of speech & devices

Figures of speech, if not labored, add greatly to the color of your seminar. We all use figures of speech without even realizing what we're doing, so they will ring comfortably in the ears of your audience.

A *simile* is a comparison of one thing to another:
"His portfolio was like a carton of broken eggs."

A *metaphor* is a comparison in which one thing is described as if it were another:
"This bawdy casino called Wall Street."

Irony says one thing to convey another:
"In an attempt to make his portfolio grow...he buried it alive."

Hyperbole is the use of exaggeration for emphasis:
"He was the best portfolio manager in the entire solar system!"

Rhyme should be used sparingly.

Anaphora is the repetition of words at the beginning of successive clauses or sentences similar to our first example in parallels...*"Stocks are best."*

Assonance is the deliberate repetition of a vowel sound, but in combination with a different consonant, so that it is not what is normally thought of as rhyme: *"old oak," "mad hat," "top notch."*

Consonance is the repetition of final consonant sounds, as in: *"tip top," "knick knack," "ding dong."*

Alliteration is the repetition of initial consonant sounds: *"deliberate, defined discipline," " tried and true," "sighted sub, sank same. "*

Cadence is rhythm combined with inflection, the melody of the phrases: *"Give me liberty or give me death. "*

There is a lot of overlapping among these categories and terms. The important thing is to grasp their function rather than to worry about what they're called.

Scrambler or pocket passer
Movement

Movement and gestures are a much maligned and misunderstood part of any presentation. Thus, they're often considered bad things. In the hands of the untrained performer, they can be dangerous. However, to a skilled seminar master, these are tools of great precision and impact. When we talk about *movement*, we're referring to your entire body. Movement of hands, arms, etc. is a *gesture*.

Movement can be fun. It helps you keep the audience's attention and can spice up a presentation. It can bring your whole body into play and allow much greater use of energetic gestures and speech patterns. It can also be distracting and tiring. I've seen speakers who oscillate from one side of the room to the other at a steady rhythm. They're like a tennis ball caught in a slow-motion baseline rally. It can actually put people to sleep.

In theater, the movement of actors is called "blocking." It is movement about the stage designed to enhance the story or create a feeling of action. There are a few questions to answer first:

1. Where are you going? Do you have a target or are you merely wandering? Wandering is not good. Better you had stayed home. Set a target point and go there.

2. Why are you going? What's the reason for the move? Are you shifting pace or themes? Are you trying to connect a thought to a previous idea? Are you sensing that they are tired and you're simply trying to wake them up? The reason or "motivation" for the movement will help answer the next question.

3. How are you going to get there? Are you going directly at a rapid pace or are you sauntering casually? Both will work depending on the message you're trying to convey. For example, you might start walking as you begin a new thought and time it so that you reach center stage at the precise moment of climax. You may want to signal a dramatic shift of mood by walking briskly to the back of the room. You might want to physically unite the crowd by starting a thought on the left side and running over to the right side to repeat the thought.

4. What are you going to do once you get there? Once you arrive at your designated spot, what's next? Do you hold that ground and deliver a few thoughts from this new locale? Are you just stopping by on the way to an even more important position? Is this a good place to begin a new thought or segment?

As you can see, movement is not haphazard. It needs to support the content. That same principle applies to gestures.

There are certain body parts (arms, legs, hands, eyes, mouth, head and torso) that can be used to convey emotion. Assuming you can exert some positive control over these appendages, you have the makings of a very expressive speaker.

What is it about some people that compels us to gesture & move when we talk. It can be a real problem. Back in my Army days, I had to give a briefing to then Vice President George Bush along with a roomful of generals. A military presentation of this nature is not the ideal venue for lots of gestures and strolling around, but I really wanted to spice things up a bit and make the talk memorable. You know, saunter out from behind the podium and casually sit on the edge of the table, Phil Donohue style. I think they would have enjoyed it and I wonder to this day what would have happened. Probably would have been court-martialed or something.

The hands

Your hands are powerful tools when it comes to gestures. They can convey many subtle meanings and messages.

The arms are a good primary tool.

"Interest rates have fallen..." Show me fallen with your hands and arms.

"The opportunity is huge..." How huge? Open your arms wide like you just caught a BIG fish.

"Move 30% of your assets overseas." Do it! Carve up an imaginary pie right in front of them and carry it across the room.

Movement and gestures give a sense of excitement and drama to the seminar. It wakes people up and gets them to focus. It also makes it more fun and it connects you to the crowd.

Keep in mind that gestures and movements walk a fine line. Too small and you look timid, powerless and unconvincing. Too grotesque and too frequent could make you look like you're having a bad reaction to some medication. You should videotape your seminars and have a friend evaluate the emotional content of your movements — first with no sound and then with sound to verify a matching image projection.

Loosen up a bit

The vast majority of speakers tend to understate their movements, so the chances are you can afford to let go a bit. As long as they support the emotional content of your message, movements can help a lot with very little downside.

If you're not comfortable with movement or gestures, you may first want to watch some professional public speakers or politicians. Keep in mind that television gestures done for the camera are totally different and much more subtle than stage movement. Your movements need to be bigger.

One of the best sources for technique on movement and gestures is those television evangelist ministers. This has nothing to do with religion, so don't go getting offended here...OK?

My favorite was Jimmy Swaggert. For all his faults, the guy was a truly an amazing speaker! He had such a range of delivery styles that you could watch him for an hour and not see the same technique twice. The hands, the eyes, the use of props, body movement, stage position, microphone technique...all coordinated with his words and perfected to drive home his emotional message. He cried, he laughed, he shouted, whispered, pounded the podium, you name it and he did it...on stage I mean. Whew, what a workout...for him AND the audience. They ate this up.

Now I don't recommend that you mimic these styles completely. There is a difference between evangelical preaching and investment seminars, if not in content, then certainly in audience expectations. If, however, you ever get a chance to drop by one of these sermons...do it. From purely a delivery point of view, I guarantee you'll learn something.

Subtle touches

There is another category of gestures you can use with great impact in a seminar. These are dramatic elements designed to communicate a subliminal message. I'm giving away some secrets here but one good example comes at the end of a presentation.

I want the audience to believe that I'm physically tired, *"drained"* as they say. I do this to convince them that I've given 110% during the seminar, which is a way of implying that I will give 110% as their financial advisor.

To convey this exhaustion I might take my glasses off and rub my tired eyes — take a deep breath to gather my strength between major thematic points — lean against the lectern, take off my jacket, un-button my tie, get a drink of water, gently mop my sweating brow.

There are a hundred of these little gestures and they can be customized to the situation. They can help you gain control, build empathy, stall for time while you're thinking, punctuate a phrase you want them to remember and loosen up a room.

Don't go crazy

The combination of vocal variety, movement and gestures definitely adds energy, excitement and enthusiasm to your seminar, but for a small percentage of you, there is a risk of going overboard. Too much excitement and you could lose credibility. If you're going to err, do so on the side of caution. Far better to have an audience walk away slightly bored than to have them thinking you're a nut job who can't stand still.

I realize that many of you will not feel comfortable with all these techniques. That's OK. If you incorporate one or two simple ideas or use a little more vocal variety, I guarantee you're not going to hurt yourself and you WILL see an improvement in audience response.

The vast majority of people doing investment seminars across the nation today are not using any of these techniques. You now have an advantage that you can use at your discretion.

CHAPTER 13

The Recap

*"Education is what you have left over after you
have forgotten everything you have learned."*
Anonymous

T ELL THEM WHAT YOU TOLD THEM. You're done with
the body of the talk and you're getting ready to move into
Q&A. Before you do that take a minute to recap. Tell them
what you told them and reinforce the logical manner in which you
analyzed the problem. The recap is vital to re-focus everyone on the
broad theme.

> *"Tonight, we looked at the economy. We examined why
> inflation and interest rates are likely to remain low for
> the next few years and then we detailed three specific
> strategies you can use right away to best position your
> portfolio for the remainder of the 90s."*

Don't skip the recap. It only takes 45-60 seconds, but it gives
the audience a chance to take a breath and make the mental transition
into the very critical Questions & Answers (Q&A) segment. A good
recap will often trigger questions they had from early portions of your
presentation. It will allow them a moment to collect their thoughts
and formulate questions.

It also allows them to begin to wind down and anticipate the end
of the event, which is a good thing since it usually relaxes them a bit.

Used properly, a recap can reinvigorate an audience and give them an attention boost for the home stretch.

The recap also allows you to insert one or two quick "factoids" that you omitted from the body of your talk. These can reinforce the image in their minds of you as the expert. It can also be a good time for a humorous story or a little levity. This adds to the relaxation process.

By the way, when I say that anticipating the end of the event is a good thing, I don't mean that they're glad you're done because you were bad or they weren't having a good time. No matter how good you are, people can only sit and listen for so long. Their brains can't take more than sixty or ninety minutes of content, even well-delivered, emotional content.

Have you ever been in a seminar kind of losing the focus, maybe drifting off mentally. Then when the moderator or speaker says *"OK only ten minutes until the break!"* you begin to perk up. *"Wow, only ten minutes...I can stay tuned in for ten minutes...then I get a break!"* And suddenly you're back into the talk.

Hey, maybe I'm the only one, who knows. Try it and see.

Finally, I use the recap to send two important non-verbal messages:

1. I am in charge here!

2. I just gave you 100% of my energy and I'm drained.

These are important concepts for a few reasons. First, you want to establish solid audience control before the dangerous Question & Answer session to follow. If you go into the Q&A with any sense of weakness or confusion, you run a greatly increased risk of enemy sniper fire.

Using the recap to reinforce the main thematic elements of your talk sets you up in a powerful light for the very important Question & Answer session to follow.

CHAPTER 14

The Q & A Session

"A coward turns away but a brave man's choice is danger."
Euripides

"It is not every question that deserves an answer."

Publius Syrus

T HE QUESTIONS & ANSWERS segment is the most dangerous part of the seminar. It's also my favorite. It exposes you to the crowd in a very direct and vulnerable position. If you screw up, you run the risk of destroying the entire emotional foundation you've established for the past 45-90 minutes. On the other hand, if you're good, you'll gain tremendous credibility and reinforce your messages. The audience will see you as someone who can move beyond any prepared text or speech and think on his feet.

The first problem is...
How to get the questions flowing

Make no mistake about it...you WANT questions. A presentation that generates questions is one that has prompted an audience to *think* not just listen. There are many things you can do throughout the seminar to assure that you get questions. You can even go so far as to plant the actual questions in their minds when a particularly tricky or controversial sub-topic is being discussed.

"Now some of you are probably wondering...why our investment discipline forced us to wait until the stock had appreciated 30% before we bought it. We can save that for the Q&A."

I will often pick out a friendly face in the crowd and give them the task of asking a specific question during the Q&A feigning that I don't want to get sidetracked at this point in the presentation. In reality, I want to use them to "shill" for me later in the event.

"OK...it's your job to remember this and ask me later! You got it?"

Then turn to the person next to them and joke...

"And it's your job to remind him!"

If you've done your job, the questions will follow very naturally. Sometimes, however, you've got to prime the pump to get the flow started. This is a very easy technique that I learned years ago. It absolutely never fails if you do it right.

When you're ready for questions, simply say *"Are there any questions?"* and raise your hand like you do in school. Keep it there for AS LONG AS IT TAKES to get a question. Maybe three seconds, maybe thirty. Even the toughest crowd, filled with people who can't wait to get to the door, will respond after 10 seconds.

The key here is to NEVER break the silence. Once you say *"Are there any questions?"*

you must not speak or move again until you get a question!

If you do as most amateurs do and say *"Oh come on. Was I that good? Did everyone understand everything?"* you release the emotional pressure and the clock starts again.

Once that first question comes out, the audience will relax and you'll probably get several hands popping up at once, otherwise simply raise your hand again... *"Any more questions?"* If it's slow, like pulling teeth, simply conclude after two or three questions. Don't drag out a painful moment. If you can't save it...let it go.

Answer briefly

Don't take forever answering the questions you DO get. This isn't a mini-seminar here. A long-winded answer is sure to make others reluctant to ask a question. In fact, your verbose style might very well be the reason you're not getting questions in the first place.

You've been in many presentations with a speaker who just went on and on. Remember how hard you prayed that it would end and that no one would ask a question. If you sense that the audience is reluctant to ask questions but someone cracks under your hand-raise pressure technique, your answer to them cannot be a ten-minute soliloquy. A quick, thoughtful response is your best chance to keep the flow going.

Some people recommend that you turn the tables on the audience and cleverly ask *them* a question. That's cute for one of those audience-participation love fests. I think audiences see right through this as a not-so-clever attempt to drag out the process. Besides, you've just spent an hour convincing them that you're the expert. All you do with this *"ask them"* technique is reduce your stature and arm a potential sniper with jacketed hollow-points.

Before you answer...you must know
The emotional context

First, you must understand a fundamental law — audiences are very sensitive about their questions. They view the Q&A as their chance to challenge and test you. Assuming you've done a good job in the body of the presentation, they will be rooting for you to pass the test, but they are eager to test you anyway. It's their God-given right and they take it seriously.

You must listen intently to the question being asked. Not only are you trying to understand the content so that you can answer appropriately, you are also trying to hear the emotional context of the question. And as you are listening, the audience is listening too. Part of your test is content. Did you answer the question being asked or did you **not listen** and answer some other question? They hate it when you do that. If you're not tuned into the question being asked, the audience will pick up on this right away. An incomplete or badly delivered answer could create feelings of unease or even disrespect...*"He's not answering that lady's question! What's the matter with him. We can't trust him!"* Bang! Just like that you've shot yourself in the gut.

Answering the right question is mainly a function of open-minded concentration. Two micro-seconds before the question begins, in that space between the time you acknowledge a raised hand and the words start to pour out of someone's mouth...you must clear your mind of noise and focus on the moment. This takes discipline, but you can do it.

While you're listening for the factual or technical content of the question, watch for clues as to the person's emotional state. Are they nervous? Probably.

— Are they angry?

— Are they probing you for truth in an effort to see if they can trust you?

— Are they trying to trip you up and show the room how much they know?

— What's the motivation for the question?

— Is it an academic issue involving some small point of discussion on which there is no right answer or...

— Is it a point of clarification on a major topic that may have confused them?

— Are you being dragged into a debate?

— Are you headed for a ride down memory lane?

What's going on here?

This emotional side is important because one person's state of mind will give you a good picture of the way many others in the room are feeling at this point. Your answer needs to be structured and delivered in such a way as to reinforce the positive emotional foundation you've built for the past hour.

In the minute or two it takes to answer the question, you may find yourself rebuilding confidence, respect, happiness, fear, the whole emotional train ride. This is what makes the Q&A so dangerous and so rewarding. You have a chance to shine brighter than you could in any other part of the event. If you do a solid job, you will have won them over totally and irrevocably.

The mechanics of
Answering questions

The process of answering questions is simple. Restate each question before you answer. Three reasons for this:

1) It shows the asker that you listened carefully

2) It gives you a chance to re-phrase the question

3) It gives you time to think

We talked about listening carefully. You know why that's important.

Re-phrasing the question is a critical step for several reasons and although it seems like it goes against what I just said about answering the question that's being asked, it doesn't.

Often the asker will present the question in such a way that the rest of the audience loses interest. You must make the question meaningful to the whole audience or you run the risk of losing control. You're going to re-phrase it so that it is interesting and still acceptable to the asker. You're going to ask permission, either verbally or through gestures to assure that your re-phrased question is OK with the asker before you answer it. Doing this does not violate the earlier rule about listening for content.

Re-phrasing the question also allows you to control the emotional sub-text. If, for example, the asker seems hostile or angry, you can bet that the audience is aware of this. You might want to relax the room or lighten him up a bit before you answer.

Often a hostile question is a prelude to a sniper attack which we'll discuss in a second. You've got to make a quick determination on how to handle this kind of question and re-phrasing allows you a moment to think and gain emotional control.

By the way, you don't always want to tone down an emotionally charged question. Sometimes it can be very powerful to build on this emotion by adding your own complimentary energy to a touchy or troubling subject.

When you're re-phrasing the question, you don't need to say *"The question was..."* Simply pause for a second, restructure and repeat the question in your own words to the entire audience. Avoid saying *"That's a good question."* It implicitly obligates you to compliment the question-askers and leaves you no room to maneuver. What do you say next? *"That's a GREAT question, That's a FANTASTIC question!"* Just skip it.

Before you leap into your answer, take a few seconds to think. Not only does this demonstrate that you're giving the question some thoughtful consideration, but it builds in "protection time" in case of a really tough question. If you think for a moment before each question, the audience won't be able to tell when you're stumped.

It's OK to direct part of the answer to the asker, but don't finish with your eyes on him. That gives them permission for a follow-up and this isn't a Presidential press conference. You want everyone to benefit from your answer and have a chance to ask their own questions and you never want to cede too much control to one individual.

What about
TOUGH questions?

Tough questions are potential trouble, but there's a specific method to handling them that should render them harmless. If you've ever done a seminar this has happened to you. Someone pops up with a question and you would absolutely swear that she just read some article in Forbes or the Economist and is asking you to comment on some detailed subject. You're at a distinct disadvantage here because the asker is armed with just enough information to sound really smart and you didn't read the article so you haven't got a clue.

Sound familiar?

Here's how you handle it.

Often, what makes the question tough is the way it was phrased. Start by re-phrasing it with your own words and try to give it a more relaxed and simplified structure. This can be done under the guise of trying to make the question more understandable to the audience who didn't read the article either, (or so you hope). What you're really trying to do is take the edge off the question — reduce the level of detail need to answer it in an intelligent-sounding manner.

Try to break a complex question down into smaller chunks and take it one bite at a time. Assuming it's a legit question and not a trap, you should have no trouble answering it and thus demonstrating your ability to think through complex situations. The audience will love this.

When confronted by a particularly tough question on a specific sub-topic that would require a detailed knowledge of items you may not be immediately familiar with, use a pyramid structure to get out of trouble. Start from a narrow focus and work down to the broader subject. Re-state the question giving it a broader perspective allowing you to answer it with a "wider view" by relating it to the main seminar theme.

I'll give you an example:

You've just done 55 minutes on global investing. It has gone very well and you feel as though the audience is eager to embrace your ideas...when suddenly...up jumps the Devil!

"According to the Economist, the decline in German unemployment will drive up inflation and interest rates in the European community. Isn't this the WRONG time to be buying foreign stocks?"

You just spent the last hour saying it was the RIGHT time to be in Europe and now this Hell Hound is destroying your credibility. What's worse is that this is a legitimate question. You *should* know the answer. It's not some obscure or irrelevant fact. All eyes are on you. You struggle. Your mind is a blur. Why didn't you read that damn article? Part of you just wants to race from the room screaming! But then your combat training takes over. You're tough and ready for anything.

"OK, let's take that one piece at a time because I want there to be absolutely no confusion on this issue."

(This re-asserts your control and confidence and subtly implies that the questioner may be confused.)

"What is the risk of rising inflation and what does that mean for the stock markets?"

(You've restated the question into a broader, less detail-driven problem.)

"In any economy there is a concern about the risk of rising inflation because, in general, that could signal higher interest rates which could put pressure on the overall stock market. These are exactly the kinds of indicators we watch every day...unemployment, productivity, wage rates, consumer prices — all of that goes into our assessment of every country's economic strength. You can't just go into these markets blindly...we've got to have solid intelligence and a good understanding of what's driving these markets and what's going to make them good long-term investments."

"We're NOT seeing any significant long-term trend in unemployment decline anywhere in Europe. The

German numbers were a three-month measurement. That's NOTHING. They didn't include any statistics on productivity or real wage increases...which are nonexistent at this point. There is no inflation anywhere in the system and the stock markets are poised for some dramatic growth. Does that mean we stop watching the indicators...not for one second. The only meaningful trends across a group of economic fronts are very positive."

"Finally, keep in mind that I am NOT recommending that you own stock in every company in every country in Europe. I am buying very selectively. We want those companies that are most likely to grow in excess of the market averages. That's the key to success."

You've handled a difficult question with calm professionalism and you've enhanced the basic premise of your theme. You did not get too deeply drawn into a discussion of German unemployment rates because you didn't know anything about them. What you knew were general facts that could be applied to any economy. You "extrapolated" from these facts and responded to the general nature of the statistics noted in the question. Did you lie? Not at all. Could you have been wrong? Sure. But no one pays you to be right ALL the time.

Even in the face of the most bizarre and obscure question this method gives you the ability to extrapolate from broad, well-defined concepts and formulate a plausible answer or explanation. When it comes to your seminar topic, there is no subject or related topic that you can't discuss intelligently for 30-90 seconds in response to a question. Or, when it gets really tough — there is no question you can't rephrase into something you DO know and CAN answer.

But keep one thought in mind — the Q&A session at the end of your seminar is not the time to solve all the world's financial problems. If you get a question that is so involved and so difficult that it will take more than one or two minutes to answer simply, or a question the answer to which would take you deep into another subject off your main thesis, gently deflect it and move on. It's not fair to the audience to make them sit through a 15 minute dialogue between you and the questioner.

"That's a very tough question. You've opened a subject that has confused many people for years and I'm not sure I can answer that in the few minutes we have left. Let me suggest that we speak after the meeting and we can spend more time on it, because it is important and I want to be able to give it some detailed attention."

I've rarely had that backfire on me. You're being very polite and straightforward. It's not that you can't answer the question but you feel it deserves a more thorough response.

Be sure, however, to follow through on this question. If you're seen trying to avoid the issue, it will have negative consequences. Immediately after the seminar, I will make a point to go right up to the person who asked the question and set a time for a meeting. *"Give me three minutes and I'll be right back here to discuss this issue. I just want to say good night to a few people."* If the asker is serious, he'll stick around and chances are you will have a small audience to hear your answer to this complex question. This can become a mini-seminar with significant benefits if you handle it well.

Is it really OK to say...
"I Don't Know?"

I have a problem here...and many of you are going to disagree with my answer. That's OK. You do it your way and I'll do it mine.

Most people will tell you that it's OK, even beneficial to say *"I don't know but I'll get back to you."* when someone asks a tough question. They say that you build trust and confidence by being honest enough to admit you don't have all the answers.

Frankly, I think that's amateur advice!

It has been my experience that the best speakers — the ones who really command respect and admiration — are never stumped by a question on their subject. I think you should ALWAYS have an answer for questions related to your topic.

There are times when you get a question from left field that has nothing to do with the subject and for which you truly do not have an answer. My solution to this is the same advice Admiral Nimitz gave to his ship captains...the first rule in freeing your ship after you run aground is...don't run aground!

Don't answer the question. No law says you have to deal with every strange question that comes up in a seminar. You're there for a reason and that's not to be a sounding board for some stream-of-consciousness rambler who needs to hear himself talk.

Casually laying out the ground rules before you start the Q&A can make this an easier task. With an undercurrent of fun and good humor, it goes something like this:

"Before we get into the questions let me set out a few rules. I've found that this helps the process and insures that everyone gets a chance to cover the issues on their mind. First...I would rather not deal with questions about individual stocks you may own. No one cares about the three shares of American Widget you inherited from your grandfather. I'll be more than happy to stay around after the seminar if you want to talk about portfolios, but not during the Q&A, OK?"

"Second...if your question takes more than two minutes to ask...it's a speech...not a question. I'm the only one who gets to make speeches here."

"Third, our topic is retirement planning, but if you have a question about a related issue...just jump right in. I know that there are many aspects of investing in general that may be confusing and that impact retirement, so if you're unclear about anything and you feel as though it's related to our subject...I want to hear from you now. I will tell you if it's too far off the subject. When I do that it usually means I don't have an answer."

You've now set the tone for the process. It's not heavy-handed or too confining. You've used humor to illustrate the common things that audiences hate during the Q&A and you've set yourself up to be able to handle anything that comes your way. By doing this, you've eliminated many of the potential *"I don't know"* responses.

I realize that this may be considered a philosophical issue. In an ideal world you would know everything about your main theme and all peripheral subjects. In the real world you must make a decision between looking less than professional by saying *"I don't know"* when you SHOULD know...or by using your vast array of experience and knowledge to "synthesize" an answer to a tough question in a public presentation environment. I claim no stake to the moral high ground. I'm a businessman like you who must make many tough decisions the net result of which are favorable to my clients.

Just when you thought you were safe...
The Q&A nightmares

But what about the really rough question or questioner? I define rough as any question or questioner which may cause me to lose the emotional edge or control of the audience.

Here are three common headaches for the Q&A part of the seminar and how to solve them.

"The Sniper"

Every crowd has one — someone who arrived with a copy of "Do-It-Yourself Investor" tucked under his arm. I'm not just talking about an honest, tough question here. Not everyone is going to agree with your thesis and a good probing question is fine. The sniper, however, doesn't really want an answer. He would rather initiate an argument and show everyone else how much HE knows. He is a potentially deadly adversary and must be terminated with extreme prejudice.

The question may be convoluted and complex. It may have nothing to do with your subject and it may come out in a fairly confrontational manner. You can feel the tension in the room rise.

Don't panic. You've got control. If you've done your job for the past hour, this audience thinks you're the expert, they like you and they are ready to side with you in battle with the sniper.

You never know when a sniper will pop up so be sure and listen to all questions carefully. The sniper gives himself away and you will be able to tell quickly that this is a potential problem. Remember, this is NOT just a good, tough question. You must be convinced that the questioner is deliberately trying to undermine your credibility before you resort to the following tactics.

Once you spot a sniper, there is a well-defined set of countermeasures that will neutralize him. Start by making a special effort to listen intently to the question with a concentrated focus on the person. Two reasons for this intense listening: First, you want to find a loophole in the sniper's logic — some faulty reasoning that you can use to deflect his fire.

Second, you want the audience to believe that you're really making an effort to understand the sniper. This will generate cooperation from them when the time is right. You want them to believe that you're truly concerned with this individual's question. Now is the time for gestures like taking off your glasses and closing your eyes or walking over toward the sniper to listen more closely. All the time you're thinking of how you're going to blow him out of the water. Isn't this fun?

While he's talking, note the effect he's having on the crowd. Are they getting nervous? Are they angry that he's taking so much time? Watch for talking, fidgeting, shuffling papers, any signs of exasperation. Do they even understand what he's asking? You need them on your side so you've got to know how they're reacting to him.

Then restate the question in very simple terms while turning away from the sniper completely. In this way you disconnect from the sniper in one physical move signaling you've had enough. Often, you can finesse an inexperienced sniper by giving a direct and brief answer to his question. But if not, never hesitate to get tough, especially if you know the rest of the room is on your side.

"That really has nothing to do with our topic tonight and I'd rather not waste everyone's time. Please see me after class."

You've been mildly forceful and used a little humor to put the sniper in his place. *"See me after class"* has a domineering ring to it that tells people you mean business.

If the sniper persists...switch to full auto...

"It seems to me that you would rather argue than ask a legitimate question, so why don't we just move on."

Or my favorite,

"I'd be more eager to give you a good answer if I thought there was the slightest chance you could understand it."

I exaggerate. It's extremely rare that you have to get that tough with anyone, but you are in command and you can't appear to lose control if you want to maintain the respect of the audience. Often, the best answer is an exasperated *"I have no idea what you're talking about!"* implying that they aren't making themselves clear or the question is so weird as to be invalid.

Using facial expressions and gestures you might want to display mild to overt annoyance at the sniper. It's a signal to your friendly forces in the audience to help out. Maybe someone sitting next to the sniper will chime in and tell him to "be quiet." Or a friendly on the other side of the room will jump up with a new question allowing you to make a clean break with the sniper. The audience dynamic when you're under sniper attack is truly amazing, and to the degree you can understand it you can control it toward your own advantage and the ultimate good of the entire room.

Whatever happens, remember this. **Never let anyone take control of your seminar.** You've spent an hour or more building an emotional state in the minds of an audience. A sniper can destroy that and negate all your efforts in a short time if you allow it. Again, I stress that we're not talking about the standard tough question. You will learn to quickly recognize the sniper over time. If you come under fire, be firm and keep control at all costs. You are 007 with a license to kill, so use it!

I Was Born In A Log Cabin...

It usually starts like this:

> *"Back in 1902, my grandfather bought 10 shares of Pacific Railroad. Now that was a good company. Why I remember a time when . . ."*

A question like this can go on for twenty minutes and can cause major gastro-intestinal distress. In an effort to be nice and to let someone talk, you could lose much of the emotional momentum you've so carefully created.

Try to avoid these kinds of personal/historical questions during the Q&A. It's just not fair to the audience. I will often prep the Q&A session with a rule, *"If you have any personal questions, I'll be happy to handle those one-on-one."* This one is easy, so be mellow, but don't waste too much time. Q&A is a very uncomfortable experience for your audience if not controlled properly.

The Unhappy Client ("The Griper")

He was *"burned by a broker"* in a partnership or a hot growth stock a few years ago and now all brokers or investment advisors are crooks and he's going to make your life miserable. This is a bad one but it can lead you into a fantastic commercial for yourself.

Try to handle his concern as honestly and openly as possible. Keep in mind that everyone in that room may have some bad experiences with a financial advisor in the past, so you can't dismiss him or treat him like a sniper (which he isn't yet). After all, there are some loose cannons in our business — a few who abuse this awesome responsibility for personal gain, just like in every profession.

At this point I will touch on my philosophy which is based on the belief that we in the financial industry have as high if not a higher moral obligation than nearly any other profession.

Take doctors for example. They take an oath that states, *"Do no harm."* We don't have that luxury. "Harm" is beyond our control because every investment involves risk, often unseen risks too. As financial professionals in a changing market environment, we must be as well versed in risk as we are in reward. Even then the best we can do is minimize potential harm...we can't eliminate it.

People usually need a doctor or a lawyer only when they're sick or in handcuffs, but people with money need us all the time. They've got to do something with it, they have no choice.

Doctors and lawyers follow universally accepted patterns of treatment or defense based on written guidelines and laws. Our laws and guidelines change every day with the markets. What was an effective "financial treatment" six months ago may be deadly to the same patient today.

In short, I believe we have a moral obligation to be more ethical, more knowledgeable and ultimately more professional than anyone who carries a title. Is that wishful thinking in this industry? Absolutely not. It's a trend very much embraced by the top practitioners in our business. What we all need to do is lead by example and continue to spread the word until everyone hears it.

Sorry — back to the unhappy client. Here's a few ideas...

"Not all investment advisors are cut from that cloth. In fact, very few. Some of us do business very differently, as evidenced by this seminar tonight. Because I know that our relationship is built on trust and that trust takes time."

> *"My clients eventually look upon me as their partner. I manage all their assets, their retirement plans, their corporate accounts and they refer me to their friends. That kind of trust is only earned over time."*
>
> *"Look, in this economic environment, anybody who owns a suit and can fog a mirror wants to advise you about your money." (PAUSE) "I try to do things differently. (PAUSE) Is it perfect? I doubt it. Is it better? Yes, absolutely. And ultimately, that's a decision that YOU make."*

I love the "Unhappy Client" because he can lead me into a powerful opportunity to sell myself very directly and very emotionally to the audience. And boy, will you have their attention, because you are mad about the way these unscrupulous brokers do business. This is one of those times when you do not want to dilute the questioner's emotional content, but rather you want to add your own emotional overtones to the answer. It would be OK for you to be even MORE angry than the questioner. This can be a great moment, use it wisely and don't be afraid.

Stream-of-consciousness know-it-alls (SOCKs)

They ramble, they tap dance, they parenthesize, they laugh at their own jokes, they tie obscure facts and incorrect data together into convoluted sentences...but under all of it there is NO QUESTION!

What SOCKs really want is to share the stage...to be up there in the spotlight with you. They're hams and they need attention. The Q&A session gives them the chance and they're going to take it.

SOCKs can be a problem particularly in club or organization seminars. They are often past presidents or persons of some influence and cannot be treated as harshly as snipers. The simplest method of dealing with a SOCK is to give them a little rope and let them hang themselves. Remember, you've still got center stage...let them talk for 20 seconds or so and once you realize they're a SOCK...simply interrupt...

> *"I'm sorry...what's the question?*

or

> *"I know there is a question in there somewhere...let me see if I can help you get to it before the next Ice Age."*

It helps to have the audience on your side, but a little humor is often all you need to reign in those loose SOCKs.

The Really Dumb Question

It has been said that the only stupid question is the one that isn't asked. That's just a polite little platitude you throw an audience who you fear may not have understood a word you've said. There are thousands of dumb questions and some will drive you crazy. *"Wasn't this person listening for the last hour?"*

As dumb as the question may be, if you *treat* it like a dumb question that audience can turn on you in a New York second. Remember, they're very possessive and sensitive about their questions. They empathize with their compadres asking the questions, so you've got to give each questioner all the respect you can muster. What does the Bible say? *How you treat the least of my brothers so shall you treat me.* Displaying patience and concern for someone who may have misunderstood a simple point will go a long way toward building respect and getting an audience to like you.

This is not to say that you must tolerate overwhelming ignorance. Again, watch the audience. If you sense that they're annoyed with the stupidity of the question being asked, you can handle it quickly and perfunctorily. If, on the other hand, they seem interested, there may be others in the audience who wanted to ask the same question but didn't have the guts. Slam dunking a dumb question could make you feel important but will usually have negative emotional results in the long run.

I've probably made the Question and Answer session seem ten times more complex than it ever did before. You figured if you just got up and gave a few good answers you'd be home free. Sorry! These last few minutes can be very important to the overall event. It's like a football team that has just marched down the field and is ready to score. The Q&A session is a first down and goal from the one yard line. Use these techniques and you will punch it in every time.

CHAPTER 15

The Finale

"Finis coronat opus."
("The end crowns the work.")
Anonymous Latin Saying

I T'S TIME TO CLOSE. Speak slowly, keep it simple, talk emotions and always end on an upbeat, positive note. Again, eye contact is critical, so memorize your close just as you did the opening.

I like the audience to think I gave 200% and now I'm drained, as if I just finished doing Richard IV. I may pause for a breath, clear my throat, mop my brow, lower my voice, take a sip of water or hold onto a chair for support. Some gesture or body position to convey that I gave maximum physical and emotional energy up there. They absolutely eat this up and it scores points. It also says that I'm the guy who gives his all for their portfolio!

"Ladies & Gentlemen, I'm very happy you came out tonight. Hopefully, you learned a few things about what's going on in the world of money. Some of you may still be a bit confused or a little scared, but that's OK. It takes years to really get comfortable with some of these concepts. Maybe we got you started on that road."

"This is a very exciting time to be an investor. There are things happening all around the world that will make the next few years very rewarding . . . and most importantly,

***YOU CAN REACH YOUR GOALS** if you're willing to take
**action.   After tonight, you're going to be better
prepared, better informed and more ready than ever to
make it happen. (PAUSE) I am here to help you. Thank
you and good night."*

Don't drag this out too long. The ending needs to be precise, not
rambling. And don't crowd the ending with administrative stuff like
collecting questionnaires or conducting the door prize drawing. If
there is anything like this that needs to be done at the end, simply
insert a line or two BEFORE the close:

*"In just a minute, I'm going to introduce my assistant,
Kristine. She's got a few announcements and she's
going to give away our door prizes."*

Then jump into your close. Let your final words be ones of
emotional, excited, professional enthusiasm.

The party's over
The post-game show

This is a very important moment in the seminar process and
there's a lot going on at the same time. People may come up to you
and want specific advice about their situation. Some may take issue
with your position on the economy. They may want to congratulate
or thank you for a wonderful evening. They might be confused about
something you said or have a follow-up question they were afraid to
ask during the Q&A session. There are many possibilities and
potential scenarios. The key is to be loose, flexible and nimble. Don't
get too deeply engaged with any one person or you risk missing the
chance to bond with the majority of the audience as they're leaving.

Trapped
Here's the scenario: You are trying to make it across the room
to shake hands with your top client who came to the seminar with a
great referral. You stop for a second and suddenly, you're surrounded
by six or seven people who want to debate your stance on inflation.
You feel like that Naval Academy Coyote who was caught in a trap
and gnawed off three of his legs but still couldn't get away.

Rule #1 — Leave yourself room to escape. Don't back into a
corner or against a wall. Stand in an open area and have clear eye
contact with your assistant in case you need help.

Free advice?

Here's the scenario: The seminar is over and you're moving to greet someone you know has some money and needs big help. You stop for a second and Daddy No-Bucks wants your opinion of his three-share stock position. What do you do? Do you blow him off and move toward the money, or do you tough it out and miss a chance to press the flesh with a half-a-mil rollover?

Rule #2 — Never get wrapped up with detailed questions from people who have no money.

This sounds terrible, but you know what I'm talking about. Sure, you should treat everyone fairly and professionally, but this is a crucial moment here. You've got some great momentum built up and it's the perfect time to shake hands with the rich and famous. Here's what you do. You calmly and sincerely say,

> *"I have found that any advice I give in a situation like this is based on incomplete data and is usually top-of-the-head commentary. What you should do if you're serious and you really want some help is to come in and see me. I really want to help you but your situation deserves more consideration than I can give it right now."*

Something like that works very well. You haven't insulted anyone and you've extricated yourself from a lengthy conversation with little profit potential. Don't conduct a private class. This isn't the forum to address every stock position or give opinions on all their concerns. If they want your concentrated effort, they've got to set an appointment. Be nice but firm about this. Any advice you dispense now isn't worth a damn anyway. You've got to review their personal situation in greater detail before you can make a recommendation.

Off the fence

Here's the scenario: Prospect X has listened intently all night but just doesn't seem ready to leap into your pocket. He comes up with a question after the seminar.

> *"Frank, what do you think of New York City municipal bonds?"*

You may or may not have any opinion on what he's asking but this is the chance to get him in for an appointment.

Rule #3 — Use Fear to give them a final push.

Here's what you say:

> *"Well, Bob (use his name) I like most of them, but muni credit analysis has gotten much more complex these days, and with all these bonds being pre-refunded (sentence fragment). . . It's nothing to worry about, but I would have your portfolio examined as soon as you get a chance."*

What did I say? Not much. What was the underlying emotional message of my words? *"You're probably going to live, but we'd better check you out just to be sure!"* Mild fear gives them the final momentum they may need to set an appointment.

Thanks for coming

If you've had a client or an important center of influence come to your seminar...go out of your way to find them during this post-game session. This is the time to cement the bond that is developing between you.

Rule #4 — Make your key attendees feel special.

This is especially true if your client brought a guest or a referral. Go up to them and greet them warmly.

> *"George...it's great to see you! I'm really glad you came tonight. Did you win a door prize? No? Don't worry, I'll have Kristine send you a dozen golf balls tomorrow!"*

Make them feel important, special, like "Big Dog" in the eyes of their friend. It will go a long way toward locking up their guest as a client and locking your client up as a source of future referrals. And besides...you are genuinely happy they came. These are your clients...your lifeblood. They deserve the best treatment you can provide 100% of the time.

In this category of "Special People to Thank" during the post-game show are any audience members you may have made fun during the seminar. If you use humor like I recommend, these people are already emotionally connected to you in a deeper way than the general audience. If you chose these people carefully, they may be your first and best clients as a result of the seminar. Meet them before they leave and thank them for their participation and great sense of humor! Offer them special help anytime they need you.

Thanks to your team

Finally, stay until the last person leaves and then give your assistants an envelope with $50 or $100 each in cash IN ADDITION to the normal overtime they are entitled to or any other financial arrangement you may have made with them.

Yes, I know it's part of their job. And yes, I know you give them a piece of the business already or a Christmas bonus...whatever. It doesn't matter. You want to tie a reward and a pleasurable experience to the actual seminar event itself. If they're good and you've used them like I've suggested throughout the planning, preparation and execution of the seminar event...they've put out a lot of extra effort. Your little gift will bond you with them in a very positive way. They will be eager to help you with your next seminar and they will be the most friendly, smiling faces in the room next time.

Remember, you're building a business here. Think like a winner!

CHAPTER 16

The Seminar Circuit

"Brother Racoons...I salute you.
Wooloo, wooloo, wooloo!"
Ralph Cramden

THESE ARE THE LIONS CLUB, THE MOOSE, The Elks, The Rotary, the Chamber of Commerce — all the groups and organizations that meet every night of the week in your community. They can be a superb source of business and community recognition as well as a powerful referral network. They are also an excellent way to develop your speaking skills. For a hundred reasons, they are a great market to target with your seminars.

In the Appendix you will find a letter and a seminar menu that I used to prospect these clubs and organizations. It's often worthwhile to pursue these groups very enthusiastically. They're filled with excellent potential clients.

The presentation techniques you use in front of such groups are a bit different than for your own seminars. They are much more like traditional speeches than full-blown seminars. The main differences are:

1. You have less time.

You're probably part of an evening's agenda with lots of other business and one or two more guest speakers. Your talk must be timed to fit their schedule. Run long and not only are you being rude to other presenters but you risk being perceived as an annoyance to the audience and perhaps getting the "hook" from the Program Chairperson. Bad form!

2. The attendees probably didn't come to hear you.

They came to hold a regular meeting and you are their weekly or monthly guest. They will be polite and courteous, but they're not likely to psychologically embrace you as quickly or as intensely as your own crowd would.

3. You're dealing with a set of pre-existing personalities.

Group behavior patterns and interpersonal hierarchies in these organizations predate your arrival by ten years. Depending on the group, it's not uncommon for members of the audience to be drunk and/or obnoxious. Some will view you as an irritant because they have important club business to discuss and you're eating into their agenda. Others will simply want to socialize with their friends and can't wait until you're done. Also, the concentration of snipers is much higher in groups like these, so you must be on your guard. Despite these risks, however, group seminars can be great fun and good business!

How best to approach
The captive seminar

The best way to deliver a presentation to a captive audience is to distill your presentation down to its emotional essence. Concentrate the key points into bullets and focus your delivery with as much power, conviction, enthusiasm and humor as you can muster.

Arrive early and mix with the crowd. This will give you valuable intelligence you can use to tailor your talk. Use the old military acronym "SALUTE" to scope out the situation.

S- Size

How big is the group? Can you deliver an informal talk or must your presentation be more structured to fit a larger audience? Do you have enough handouts? Is this group part of a national organization with referral opportunities for future presentations?

A- Activity

What are they doing prior to your presentation? Are they covering serious group business or are they simply socializing. Is alcohol flowing freely? What kind of conversations are they having?

Are they talking about you and your presentation or another speaker's? Is there any group event or characteristic that you can refer to in your talk either for humorous bonding or to enhance a serious part of your discussion?

L - Location

What's the facility like? Are you speaking from a lectern or can you walk around? Are there any distractions? Are waiters scurrying around and making noise or is a meeting going on next door? Can they see and hear you from all points in the room? Are the lights and temperature comfortable or will you have to contend with environmental problems? Where are the exits? (Not for a hasty retreat, but to know where to position yourself after the event to insure maximum traffic flow and individual contact.)

U - Unit

This is a military term but in simple, civilian language: who *are* these people? Prior to the event, you should do some research. When was the group founded? What do they do? Do they have any famous members? Showing a group that you know something about them is a powerful strategy for getting them to like you.

At the event itself you can get more information. I want to get a feel for the kind of personalities in the group. Are they conservative and stodgy or are they a fun-loving crowd likely to respond well to humor? Who are the formal and informal leaders? Who can you make fun of and who should you avoid? Who has money and may warrant some special focus?

T - Time

You will probably know the agenda prior to the meeting, but there may have been changes. Can you expand your talk or must you cut it short? Your "feel" for the audience may also dictate changes in presentation length. For example, you may learn that they *never* have two speakers at the same meeting but tonight they've gotten a surprise visit from their National Chapter Imperial Grand Poobah and he may say *"a few words"* after you're done. They may all be anxious to hear him speak. Go too long and you might make them uncomfortable whereas cutting your talk a bit short would almost certainly garner you recognition as a perceptive professional and might get you back for a follow-up visit.

E- Equipment

Is there a microphone and does it work? If you're using visuals, is there appropriate AV equipment? You've probably come prepared with certain visual aids but you may have gotten bad information. That slide projector last saw action in 1961. The VCR is Beta. You should be able to switch between formats from slides or overheads to a flip chart presentation at will. If you're bringing your own equipment, where are the electrical outlets and extension cords?

"Cry havoc and loose the dogs of war."
Be the last speaker

Too bad Brutus went first. It would have gone a lot better for him if he could have grabbed the crowd with a few jokes at the end of Antony's speech...

> *"Let's hear it for Marc Antony...you know that reminds me of a story. A man walks into the Senate with three dogs...a Poodle, a German Shepard and a Dachshund..."*

With very few exceptions, it's usually best to be the last speaker on the program. The audience will remember best what they hear last. In nearly every forum, the main attraction is the final speaker on the program. Simply being the final speaker will often lend credibility and stature to your presentation.

Going last is also an advantage in situations where the agenda includes only one combined question and answer session at the end of the event. By going last, you usually generate more questions because you're freshest on their minds. You should tailor the end of your talk specifically to generate these follow-up questions.

The risk of going last is timing. If the first speaker takes too much time, you may find yourself cut short. There are few things I hate worse than when the Program Chairperson allows the first speaker to ramble on and then introduces me by saying, *"We're a little short of time, so if you could hurry it up a bit..."*

It takes all my self-control to stop from grabbing a butter knife and pinning his sleeve to the table Luca Brazzi style. ***"Hey pal, I drove two hours to be here, so you just sit down and relax 'cause I'm talkin' now!"***

Of course, there's a better way to handle this.

There are only three times when going first is better:

1 — If you sense that the audience is likely to get impatient or restless with the length of the agenda as planned such as when the Grand Poobah comes to town and will be speaking after you're done.

2 — If you know the other speaker is likely to go long and cut into your time.

3 — If the other speaker is a lot better presenter than you. It's always hard to follow a polished pro. Even though a real pro would never intentionally blow you out of the water, they can't help it. The ability differential will cause you to look much weaker than you would against ordinary competition. Best to do your thing, make it powerful, sit down and learn from a master. Some day that will be you!

> *The one caveat to this is what I call "The Seinfeld Effect." Any TV show following Seinfeld is usually a major hit as well. Once, I was speaking at a major event and was slated to follow a nationally famous motivational speaker. I attended his meeting in hopes of picking up clues as to the mindset of the audience. It worked like a charm. I was able to quickly re-tailor my opening delivery style to complement and contrast the other speaker's style. The end result was a major hit with the crowd. The success of his "warm-up act" made my presentation shine even brighter!*

If there are additional speakers on the program, you need to know what they're going to talk about. If it's another financial planner, someone just like you, always go last! If you're scheduled to go first, get with the Program Chairperson and make up some excuse like *"I have to be on a special conference call with our office in Indonesia at exactly 8:00 PM. It will only last fifteen minutes but could you perhaps re-arrange the order of presenters and let me go last?"*

Time the delay to put you back in the room just after the first speaker has begun. You don't want to miss his presentation, because you're going to watch the crowd's reactions and build on his ideas. The program people usually don't mind the change, and this little ruse lets you land the emotional knock-out punch.

Unique aspects of
Club & organization seminars

There are a couple of things to watch out for at these "mammal" seminars. (The Elk, Moose, Lions, Raccoons etc.) One is hecklers. You can't handle a group heckler the same way you handle a "sniper" during your own seminar. Verbally vivisecting someone may work just fine when it's *your* crowd, but when you're the guest...they don't take kindly to that kind of massacre.

The best way to handle a situation like this is to have a few quick-witted comebacks ready for non-lethal delivery if a heckler gets out of hand. Basic stuff like:

> *"I guess the wife is away for the week."*

> *"OK no more prune juice for Harry over here!"*

Chances are the group knows who the trouble makers are. They probably pop off at every meeting and no one takes them too seriously. What will be judged is your ability to handle them with firm but gentle humor. Do it well and they will like you. Smack old Harry too hard...and you risk having the group turn on you.

Eating

Very often there will be some kind of food served at these events. The basic rule of public speaking is: **Do not eat anything thirty minutes before you speak.** The reason for this is spit...saliva. Eating causes a build-up of saliva that lasts some time after you finish eating. This forces you to clear your throat a lot which is very distracting to the audience. Some foods are worse than others. Dairy products like milk, cheese or chocolate are forbidden. You'll sound like you're drowning.

If you are there for dinner before you speak, eat lightly and avoid the trouble foods. No one will mind and it will make for a better presentation. Also, be aware that the audience is eating and expect some heavy duty throat clearing if they're doing a lot of dairy or sweets. Normally, this chortling is a sign that they're losing interest in your talk, but after a big meal, they can't help it.

Handouts

It's not as easy to use complex handouts at a mammal seminar as it is with your own crowd. If anything, keep your handout to one page and keep it non-sales oriented. You might want to have your business card data somewhere on the handout. If you are talking about specific investments you might need to have prospectuses. Place them on a table in the back and refer to them but don't hand them out.

"Folks, I'm required by SEC regulations to make the prospectus available for you. I've placed these on a table in the back of the room so please feel free to take one on your way out."

Have your business card stapled to the sales kit.

Use of humor is more important

As important as humor is in a regular seminar, it's more important in a mammal seminar. Two reasons:

1. This is a group of people who get together on a regular basis and who know each other as friends in addition to group colleagues. This places them into a more entertainment-oriented mindset.

2. You're dealing with an experienced audience here. They are a regular stop on the regional speaker circuit and they hear many different kinds of speakers from professional politicians to raw amateurs. They expect a certain humorous delivery and content and will respond to humor very well.

This is not to say that you can't have a serious message. You can! But be aware that these kinds of groups enjoy a good laugh more than a typical seminar audience. You simply need to increase the humor content in your presentation by one or two notches.

If that causes you concern, there is another alternative. Rather then upping the humor level, increase the drama level. Give them something to get emotionally involved with as an audience. Be more insightful, dynamic and energetic.

Use a greater degree of vocal variety. Make some bold, compelling, even controversial statements and add impact to your message. Give them a little theater.

The best analogy I can think of is on Broadway. What do the tourists and the first-time theater goers all want to see? *Cats!* An experienced Broadway aficionado wants more. They need more substance from the experience to make an impression. That's what these groups are like. At least being aware of the need beforehand will arm you to prep your talk a little differently.

CHAPTER 17

Generating Attendance

"Whatsoever thy hand findeth to do, do it with thy might."
Ecclesiastes

A LL THE TALENT, PREPARATION, speaking skill and content on earth is meaningless if only three people show up to your seminar. Generating attendance is a vital first step in the seminar process — and it's easy!

Five simple steps

Getting people to show up is a five-step process that will guarantee you great attendance every time. There are minor variations on this process and *everyone* has an opinion on how to get people to come to a seminar. If you've got a technique that's working, don't even THINK of changing it. If you can consistently pack a roomful of 30-50 people every month or every two months, you're on your way to a monster business (assuming you do all the other stuff in the book as well).

The formula allows for a good deal of flexibility depending on the demographic market you're in, the type of seminar you're doing and the target audience, but the essentials are common to all events. The key is to DO IT. This is where the process breaks down. You say you're going to call everyone on the list and you stop after reaching four or five. You plan to send your tickets a week in advance and you get them out the day before the event. The formula works if you do. If not, you're in the laps of the Gods.

Attendance Formula: Step 1:
Find a good location

It's like real estate...location, location, etc. A good location is defined as an upscale facility at the geographic center of an area with a five minute driving radius of your target audience. Why a five minute radius? Because one hour before the event is when you lose the most people. That's the moment they're making the "Go/No Go" decision. If they have further than five or maybe ten minutes to travel, you're percentage of dropouts will increase...particularly in inclement weather environments.

If you're doing a seminar primarily for new prospects, the five minute rule should hold firm. If, however, you're targeting existing clients, they probably don't live within five minutes of any single spot, so the five minute driving criteria may be too restrictive. Even so, the facility should be as centrally located and as easy to get to as possible for the bulk of your people.

The facility can be a hotel, a country club, a library, a restaurant, a theater, a conference center, a school room...any place that's clean and pleasant with tables and chairs and room for you to set up your visual aids. Depending on the image you're trying to project, you might lean more towards the higher quality sites on the list. Typically that's a conference center or a nice hotel, although I've been in public libraries that were really great as well.

An ideal location would be easy to find, have plenty of free parking and be relatively free of distractions. I did a seminar at a gorgeous country club in Las Vegas. Everything was great except that the room had windows that opened out onto the first tee. On a busy Saturday morning, this can be a hectic visual scene with which to compete.

Obviously, the ideal facility should fit within your budget. I would be willing to allocate up to 30% of the cost of the total event to the facility. That would be where I felt that the facility itself was a selling point to the seminar such as at a swanky private country club or a nice restaurant. Now location can help boost your attendance.

Attendance Formula: Step 2
Pick an exciting topic

We could argue this issue forever, so let me share my simple philosophy and leave you to decide on what's right for you.

The purpose of a seminar is to do what? To sell yourself!

Some will say "to educate" my clients. That's fine. But what you're really trying to do is to sell them on the image of you *as an educator* and how that makes you better than other financial advisors. Be honest...you know I'm right.

Given that your goal is to create or enhance your own image in the minds of your audience...you should pick a topic that allows you to really shine — something that gives you a chance to look really smart and to fully portray those best aspects of your business practice. That means you should...

Pick a topic that gets YOU excited!

If you're fired up about something, the odds are excellent that you will be able to get an audience fired up too.

This may not work all the time. If, for example, you're doing a multi-session seminar where you're going to cover a broad range of financial topics over a few weeks, it might include stuff like muni bonds or insurance or other traditionally "boring" areas. There are two alternatives here.

One: find something in your "boring" topics to get excited about. There is no subject area within the broad category of investing that cannot be brought to life with a little historical knowledge, research or creativity. Everything about this business has some element of excitement in it. Find it and use it. Do not allow money and investing to become mundane or trivial, especially in a seminar presentation.

Two: if you really think that a topic is boring and you can't come up with any sizzle, try to match it up with others that *are* exciting. This creates an agenda in which each event has some sizzle. Do NOT lump all of your boring topics into one presentation. You'll drive them into a coma.

Use the media to support and publicize

The ideal topic should not only be exciting but timely. It helps tremendously to have some recent press discussing your theme. Your chances of getting a SRO crowd really go up when your theme is on the front pages and you can send a recent news or magazine article with your invitation. The media can definitely help you pack a room, so seek out sources that support your seminar effort and use them.

As for publicity, you must create your own excitement. Send out press releases, invitations to local media luminaries, sample audio tapes with soundbites from past seminars and articles for publication. Understanding how the media works will help you to work with it in publicizing your events. Take a reporter to lunch and learn about their pressures and challenges. These are professionals with a job to do and to the extent that you can help them do it...you will be helping yourself.

Should you vary the topics?

Let's think about this for a second. Suppose you've found a target audience with good client potential. Your mailing list contains roughly 5,000 names. You've contacted them about a seminar on a strong theme like Global Investing. Chances are you've reached less than 20% of your potential audience with your initial invitation. Of that 20% who actually saw your invitation, you might have gotten a 10% hit rate, which means 2% of your total target audience actually RSVP'd to your seminar.

If I were you, barring extraordinary circumstances, I would try the same seminar five more times over the next year within that target group or until your RSVP rate dropped below one half of one percent. In other words, when you send out 5,000 invitations to a qualified prospect list and fewer than 25 people respond, that would signal the time to change topics.

Notice I said "respond." If you're using a reply-card type mailer, this may mean that they simply requested information, NOT that they actually showed up to the seminar.

As you know, the key to advertising is repetition, but there's an added benefit of doing the same seminar several times within the same market. You begin to build your reputation as an expert on a specific topic. This is another reason I suggest picking a rich topic. Who cares if you're an expert on mortgage derivatives. That's too narrow to do you any real good. But if you're an expert on GROWTH INVESTING IN THE NEW ECONOMY...or AVOIDING THE COMING RETIREMENT CRISIS...you've got a broad bandwidth over which you can deliver lots of value for a long time.

The other benefit of repetition is that you really start getting good. After one or two seminars, you will begin to notice the audience's reactions to your various delivery styles and content elements. These are things you probably would never see early on because you're too concerned about doing the presentation. After a while, the presentation becomes more comfortable and familiar. This allows you the freedom to expand or alter selected portions of content or delivery in order to achieve maximum audience impact.

Attendance Formula: Step 3
Sell the seminar with enthusiasm

This begins with the initial written invitation.

What format of invitation generates the best results and most positive feelings? I have given this a lot of thought and study and I cannot draw any definitive conclusions. As long as the invitation is interesting and easy to read and respond to, there are a wide variety of formats that will work.

I've used them all from wedding style to multi-page letters to hand written notes to fliers on fluorescent yellow paper. My personal favorite for many reasons, is the double-sided, tri-fold reply mailer. seen on the next two pages. This gives you plenty of room for all pertinent event information. It allows the placement of endorsements on the outside flap opposite the address panel so they can be read without opening the piece. The reply mailer will generate leads even from people who cannot attend and it can be customized to reflect specific areas of my interest at the time.

These kind of mailers are easy to design and print (including the reply mail bar-coding) with any type of desktop publishing software including Quark Express, Corel Ventura or PageMaker. With a little skill, you or your assistant can crank these out with ease, saving the cost of expensive typesetting.

The reply mailer MUST be postage paid. In some cases, I might use a reply envelope, but this is one more step that significantly bumps up the cost of your postage and supplies. Simplicity and ease

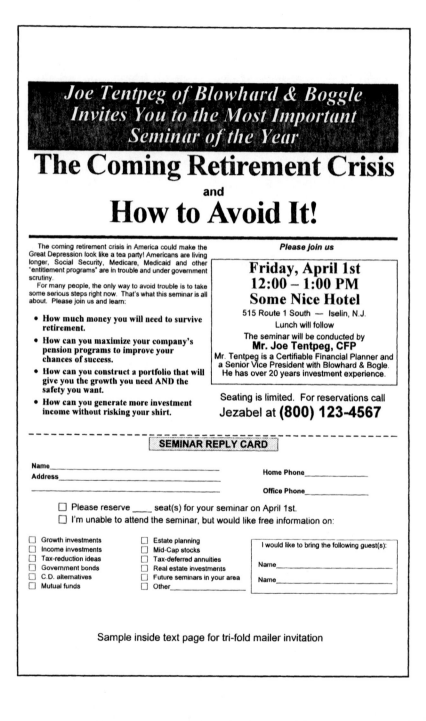

Joe Tentpeg of Blowhard & Boggle Invites You to the Most Important Seminar of the Year

The Coming Retirement Crisis
and
How to Avoid It!

The coming retirement crisis in America could make the Great Depression look like a tea party! Americans are living longer, Social Security, Medicare, Medicaid and other "entitlement programs" are in trouble and under government scrutiny.

For many people, the only way to avoid trouble is to take some serious steps right now. That's what this seminar is all about. Please join us and learn:

- **How much money you will need to survive retirement.**
- **How can you maximize your company's pension programs to improve your chances of success.**
- **How can you construct a portfolio that will give you the growth you need AND the safety you want.**
- **How can you generate more investment income without risking your shirt.**

Please join us

Friday, April 1st
12:00 – 1:00 PM
Some Nice Hotel

515 Route 1 South — Iselin, N.J.
Lunch will follow

The seminar will be conducted by
Mr. Joe Tentpeg, CFP
Mr. Tentpeg is a Certifiable Financial Planner and a Senior Vice President with Blowhard & Bogle. He has over 20 years investment experience.

Seating is limited. For reservations call
Jezabel at **(800) 123-4567**

SEMINAR REPLY CARD

Name_____
Address_____
_____

Home Phone_____
Office Phone_____

☐ Please reserve ____ seat(s) for your seminar on April 1st.
☐ I'm unable to attend the seminar, but would like free information on:

☐ Growth investments
☐ Income investments
☐ Tax-reduction ideas
☐ Government bonds
☐ C.D. alternatives
☐ Mutual funds

☐ Estate planning
☐ Mid-Cap stocks
☐ Tax-deferred annuities
☐ Real estate investments
☐ Future seminars in your area
☐ Other_____

I would like to bring the following guest(s):
Name_____
Name_____

Sample inside text page for tri-fold mailer invitation

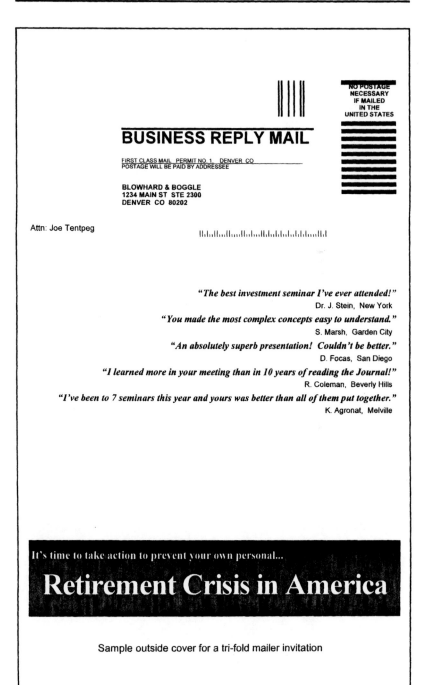

BUSINESS REPLY MAIL

FIRST CLASS MAIL PERMIT NO. 1   DENVER CO
POSTAGE WILL BE PAID BY ADDRESSEE

BLOWHARD & BOGGLE
1234 MAIN ST STE 2300
DENVER CO 80202

NO POSTAGE
NECESSARY
IF MAILED
IN THE
UNITED STATES

Attn: Joe Tentpeg

"The best investment seminar I've ever attended!"
Dr. J. Stein, New York
"You made the most complex concepts easy to understand."
S. Marsh, Garden City
"An absolutely superb presentation! Couldn't be better."
D. Focas, San Diego
"I learned more in your meeting than in 10 years of reading the Journal!"
R. Coleman, Beverly Hills
"I've been to 7 seminars this year and yours was better than all of them put together."
K. Agronat, Melville

It's time to take action to prevent your own personal...

Retirement Crisis in America

Sample outside cover for a tri-fold mailer invitation

of reply are the key elements here. There will be times when a more elaborate invitation approach is called for, but why pay for 5,000 reply envelopes when the whole thing can be self-contained in one piece?

The wedding style invitation (below) is popular with what I call "high-brow" seminars like Money Management or Estate Planning.

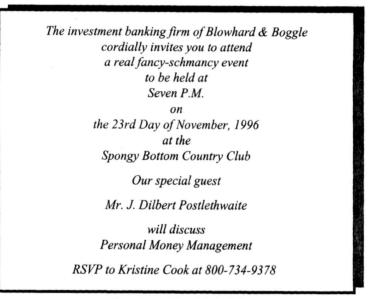

The investment banking firm of Blowhard & Boggle
cordially invites you to attend
a real fancy-schmancy event
to be held at
Seven P.M.
on
the 23rd Day of November, 1996
at the
Spongy Bottom Country Club

Our special guest

Mr. J. Dilbert Postlethwaite

will discuss
Personal Money Management

RSVP to Kristine Cook at 800-734-9378

Sample wedding-style invitation.

I guess some people like the sophisticated feel and think it lends credibility to the event. If that works for you, use it.

You should include a toll-free 800 number for responses. Here again, make it easy and free for them to respond. Be certain that the person answering the phones knows all the details of the seminar. You will defeat your emotional purpose if they call in and are transferred twice or put on hold for 5 minutes while simply trying to reserve a seat.

In an ideal world, the person taking these calls would say something like...

"Thanks very much for calling...I'm sure you're going to enjoy the seminar!"

But I know that's a lot to ask these days, so forget it. I could easily make the case for hiring a good answering service to take these incoming calls. For the feel of maximum professionalism, they will add much to your pre-event staging.

The initial follow-up call

Selling the seminar also takes place during the follow-up phone call and it is a sales presentation as well-thought-out as any you would make for a hot growth stock or mutual fund. This means talking about the benefits of attending, not just the cold facts of date and location. You're asking these people to invest their time and you've got to tell them why it's important. I'm NOT talking "hard sell," just a confident enthusiasm worthy of a high-class event.

I would stress three key points in this sales "pitch."

- You're going to pick up lots of timely, high-quality investment intelligence that you can't get in other places or from other people.
- There will be no sales pressure...this is strictly an educational service that you provide to the community a few times a year.
- You will have fun and be entertained by an excellent speaker.

If you're using callers to do the follow-up, test them for enthusiasm, energy level and ability to tell a compelling story. Your seminar is special — it's better then any other event in the area. The people you hire to spread the word must be convinced of that and be convincing to others.

Use humor to coax them off their butts

"Mr. Jones...I know you could be home watching Bay Watch...but this is a lot more stimulating...in *most* ways."

A little relaxed humor during the follow-up implies that the event itself will be enjoyable too. Have fun with this. Think of it as inviting a group of friends to your home for a party.

"By the way...we're going to have the best little cheese cubes you've ever tasted. They're being flown in special from Wisconsin that afternoon."

Never press too hard. This is obvious. If you're getting nowhere with someone, be polite and move on. You always want the ability to go back for a future seminar and you never, NEVER want to make anyone angry or make them feel as though you're hungry for business. These are exclusive events and you've got a thousand people who can't wait to attend!

Assume the sale

Another approach to the initial follow-up call is to assume they're coming.

> "Mr. Jones, I was just calling to confirm your reservation and to see if you're planning to bring any guests. We've had a cancellation and we've got room for one more if you have a friend you'd like to bring."

This is a technique I usually reserve for the final confirmation call, but it can work well as an initial follow-up call too. Typically the response is bewilderment and you can pretend that you got erroneous information... *"but now that there's an opening anyway..."*

Attendance Formula: Step 4
Send everyone a ticket

Often overlooked, a ticket is an important physical link to the event (see next page). It should have all the pertinent seminar information on it including directions to the facility. It should also have a unique Raffle Number on it. This will be used in the awarding of the door prize. Have I talked about door prizes yet? No? Well, have some!

People like to get free stuff. If it comes down to a last minute decision between your seminar and a re-run of Three's Company, this might just put them over the top.

You can be as creative as you wish. I usually go for books, golf umbrellas or balls, subscription to financial magazines or any of the hundreds of little giftie items you have available to you. These make the event fun and ensure that you will get everyone's name and address before they depart.

The ticket should arrive one week to ten days before the event. You should include one for each *person*, not each couple. You should

Sample Seminar Ticket: Side One

Sample Seminar Ticket: Side Two

also include one extra for a guest. This gives you a good reason to confirm with them on the day of the event.

One added touch I've seen done is to send a magnetic business card with the tickets. This gets them right onto the refrigerator door.

Attendance Formula: Step 5
Call to confirm

When? **The day of the event!** Not *three days* before or even *the day before*. The day OF! The only exception to this is if you're doing a breakfast seminar where you'd call the night before.

This is the final shove that will move them out the door when the moment arrives. Calling the same day reduces no-shows to a bare minimum. You have done all you can do. If they don't post now, you have tacit permission to be pissed off and chances are high that you can close them on an appointment when you call to *"...find out what happened."* The final call is where you could go into your *"we had one cancellation..."* routine. You can also confirm the guest.

That's it folks. Five easy steps to filling your seminar.

- Pick a good location
- Pick a timely topic that excites you
- Sell the seminar with enthusiasm
- Send a ticket
- Call the day of the event to confirm

Please don't make this process any more complex than it really is. I mean, let's just cut the crapola. I've found, the majority of the time, when a broker or advisor complains about the difficulty of generating attendance, it usually turns out that they're only half-hearted about the seminar. They're going through the motions. They're not really into it. Someone told them that it might be a good idea, they've got a wholesaler coming in, paying for the event, they've got an untrained caller doing the inviting...overall a weak effort.

If that's you...now's your chance to change. It's time to *"fish or cut bait"*...to *"_____ or get off the pot."* Those are the only two cliches that spring to mind, but you get the message.

CHAPTER 18

Stage Fright

*"It's not that I'm afraid to die. I just don't want to
be there when it happens."*

Woody Allen

I have this recurring dream. It must be an actor's nightmare. Here I am standing backstage of a major theatrical production. I've got a leading role and it's seconds before my entrance. Suddenly I realize that I can't recall any of my lines. I'm frantically grabbing for a script and trying to memorize my lines for this crucial scene...but it's hopeless...there's no time...I'm on and no words will come out. Then I wake up.

What do you think it means, Doc?

The biggest and the best still get...
Butterflies

If you're nervous about public speaking, you're not alone. It is one of the greatest fears people have, ranking right up there with death and IRS audits. You are probably not in that group who quivers, shakes, vomits or faints at the thought of having to stand up in front of a group of people and speak, but you might still have a few butterflies.

Please believe me — ALL speakers get butterflies. They never go away totally. I don't know a single person who doesn't get a little twinge just before they go on. There is a nervous energy involved with the act of public speaking that manifests itself in a very physical way. It's different for each person but you can feel it in your gut.

This is a normal level of anxiety and it becomes much less noticeable after you've had some experience. Beyond this, however, is a deeper fear — a certain type of public speaking tension that usually comes from two main sources: **"Administrative or Presentation Anxiety."**

"Administrative Anxiety" is easily avoided by being totally organized. "Presentation Anxiety" can only be overcome by solid preparation and mastery of the techniques we're discussing in this book. Fears like *"What am I going to say?" "What if I forget something important or make a mistake?" "What if they ask me something I can't answer?"* are very controllable and quickly dispersed with the confidence that comes from having delivered your talk a few times.

Some people will tell you to picture the audience naked, or some other mental trick like that. Frankly, that can be too complicated or distracting. Instead, use this checklist to help you overcome stage fright.

REDUCING ANXIETY

1. Organize

Lack of organization will kill you. It will sap your emotional strength and reduce your effectiveness dramatically. Knowing that your thoughts are well organized and that your presentation flows smoothly from one point to the next in a logical fashion will give you more confidence, which will allow you to focus on your presentation and the delivery of ideas.

2. Visualize

Imagine walking into a room, delivering your presentation with enthusiasm, fielding questions with confidence and leaving the room knowing you did a great job. Mentally rehearse this sequence with all the details of your particular situation, and it will help you focus on what you need to do to be successful.

Visualization may sound corny, but every great athlete, especially the ones who compete in mentally intensive sports like tennis or golf, will tell you that success visualization plays a major role in their training, pre-game preparation and actual game execution.

3. Practice

Many speakers rehearse a presentation mentally or with just their lips. Instead, you should practice standing up, as if an audience were in front of you, and with your visual aids (if you have them). At least two dress rehearsals are recommended. If possible, have somebody critique the first one and/or have it videotaped. There is no better preparation than this.

4. Breathe to relax

When your muscles tighten and you feel nervous, you may not be breathing deeply enough. The first thing to do is to sit up, erect but relaxed and inhale deeply a number of times. Instead of thinking about the tension, focus on relaxing. As you breathe, tell yourself on the inhale, *"I am"* and on the exhale, *"relaxed."* Proper breathing will get those butterflies in your stomach to all fly in one direction and it will give you an oxygen boost to clear your head and increase alertness.

5. Release tension

As tension increases and your muscles tighten, nervous energy can get locked into the limbs. This unreleased energy may cause your hands and legs to shake. Before standing up to give a presentation, it is a good idea to try to release some of this pent up tension by doing a simple, unobtrusive isometric exercise. Starting with your toes and calf muscles, tighten your muscles up through your body finally making a fist. Immediately release all of the tension and take a deep breath. Repeat this exercise until you feel the tension start to drain away.

6. Move

Speakers who stand in one spot and never gesture experience tension. In order to relax you need to release tension by allowing your muscles to flex. If you find you are locking your arms in one position when you speak, then practice releasing them so that they do the same thing they would if you were in an animated one-on-one conversation. You can't gesture too much if it is natural.

Moving with your feet is important as well. You should take a few steps, either side-to-side or toward the audience. When speaking from a lectern you can move around the side of it for emphasis. Don't hide behind it. If you're comfortable, you can move throughout the audience. When tied into the context of your presentation, this level of dramatic movement adds a bold tone to the event.

7. Make eye contact with the audience

Remember the "Audience Mind Meld." Make your presentation similar to a one-on-one conversation. Relate with your audience as individuals. Look in people's eyes as you speak. Connect with them. Make it personal and personable. The eye contact should help you relax because you become less isolated from the audience and learn to react to their interest in you. Their enthusiasm will encourage you and the effect is very positive.

8. Listen to radio talk shows on money

One of the best ways to develop confidence in your expertise is to hear for yourself how little the investing public knows about the world of money and how desperate they are for good information. This will also remind you to structure your presentation so that it's understandable to the public, not a roomful of portfolio managers.

Whenever I'm nervous, I remember listening to a radio call-in program on investing. I have a vivid recollection of the questions being asked by the public and how basic they were. These people were obviously motivated enough to actually call a radio show, so I assume they felt that their problem was important. I remember listening to this program thinking how little the public knows about investing — even the largest and most sophisticated investors know virtually nothing except their own portfolio and investment history.

This thought has helped me in speaking situations that would drive most financial professionals insane. I once spoke before the San Diego Chapter of the American Association of Individual Investors. These are the "one-cent centurions"— people who trade with the deep discounters for a penny a share. They truly think that they're smarter than most brokers. I wondered, *"What in God's name am I going to tell these people? How am I going to impress them given their level of knowledge and understanding?"*

On the way to the seminar I tuned into one of those radio talk-shows, purely by accident. It was inspiring. It left me with the unqualified confidence that compared to "the public" I was Warren Buffett! The feeling was extraordinary and I blew the audience away.

CHAPTER 19

Visual Aids

"We are as much as we see. Faith is sight and knowledge. The hands only serve the eyes."

Henry David Thoreau

T here are many ways to present seminar information visually. These range from high-tech, computer-generated, multi-media shows to low-tech chalk on a blackboard. Each has advantages and drawbacks, some of which may surprise you. Let's take these in reverse order of my personal preference.

SLIDES

We've all been to hundreds of presentations where slides were the main visual aid. They are the bread and butter of investment seminars. Everybody uses them...and they could be killing you!

It's highly likely that many of you will be using pre-packaged seminars created by the marketing department and ninety percent of the time they'll give you slides. So here you are happily clicking away with the remote control thinking you're doing a seminar. You're not!

What you're doing is reading to them from the slide. Gee, can't they read for themselves? Of course! Then why do they need you? Good question.

If all you do is click slides, you're not likely to make it big with seminars. You've got to do more — much more. You've got to enhance, expand and energize the commentary on and between each slide with your own words. The problem is, that no matter how good you are, or how much energy you're putting out, they are still looking at the screen. It becomes direct competition for their attention and can actually reduce the level of understanding in their minds.

When you use slides, you may find that the most powerful thing you can do during the seminar is to TURN THE SLIDE PROJECTOR OFF and simply talk through a concept. It's exciting and it will improve your results dramatically.

Slides: Pros

- ### Multi-color/high resolution looks great

  Slides can display a wide variety of complex and exciting visual images. They offer photo-quality resolution and can support your talk with charts and graphs that are easy-to-see from the back row.

- ### Professionally designed by marketing

  Typically, someone other than you is preparing the slides for a seminar presentation. That means you rarely have to worry about compliance issues.

- ### Easy to carry and set up

  The typical slide projector is totally self contained and you can also use a wireless remote control.

- ### Requires little mental effort

  If you're pressed for time, all you have to do is click the clicker. The real seminar pro will use only selected slides and not allow the slide show to become the main presentation. Also, they will master the transition points between each slide.

Slides: Cons

- ### Projector costs money

  Even a low-end slide projector will run you $350 to buy or $100 to rent from a seminar facility. Your office may have one, so this may not be an issue for many.

- ### Impersonal

  Slides have a tendency to dominate the event. They become the show instead of you. The audience is focused on the screen and you have to compete for their attention. Also, people know that you did not create the slides, thus you become more of a "reader" rather than a true expert.

- ## No design or content input

  You may have absolutely no control of the look or content of the slide show except to edit out those individual slides you don't like. Often, slides are poorly designed with the disclaimers on the bottom taking up more room that the main chart. You're stuck.

- ## Techno-failure possible

  A dead slide projector is a cold enemy. It leaves you little recourse and usually ill-prepared for improvisation. Are you ready? OK then here it is...BRING AN EXTRA BULB! Whew, I was waiting for that.

OVERHEADS

Overheads have most of the same benefits and drawbacks as slides with one major exception — you can make your own! To make your own slides cost big bucks: even after the design work it can run $10 per slide. Home-based slide production is very rare. Overheads, on the other hand, are a breeze to make. And the visual quality is good — not as good as slides, but very reasonable especially with a good color printer.

Overhead Pros

- ### High quality possible

  If you're doing your own overheads, you can get near-photo quality, or 720 DPI output from a color ink-jet printer. These will be very readable and colors will look great giving you virtually the same visual support capability as a slide show.

- ### Can be home-grown

  Overheads require only a printer and transparency paper to create an entire slide show. Now you can control the design and content of your visuals within compliance guidelines.

  If you're making color overheads on an ink-jet printer, you can't use the typical transparency paper found lying around in most office supply rooms. You will find that the ink smears and drips right off. Instead, you need special transparency sheets which cost roughly $60 for a 50-sheet pack. Follow the directions carefully, because they need to dry before they can be handled.

- ### Can be copied into hand-outs

  Substitute regular paper and you've got a hand-out set for the audience.

- ## Create the visual for large audiences.

  For big rooms, where a flip chart is not practical, you can still
  create the visual right on the overhead transparency.

  One of the best presentations I've seen was given using partially
  prepared overheads. This gave the speaker something more than a
  blank page to work with (which can be scary if you ever lose your
  train of thought), but still allowed him to create the visual. Each
  overhead had a title or part of a graph already drawn. It saved lots of
  time and seemed to work very well. It also created a little excitement
  as he filled in items on a blank pie chart, for example. But then I'm
  easily excited anyway.

Overhead Cons

- ## You still need a projector

  Most overhead projectors are bulky and heavy. Not the kind of
  thing you want to lug around to your seminars. But they are
  easy to rent and cost about the same as a slide projector.

- ## Still a bit impersonal

  Less so than slides, especially if you've designed them yourself,
  but they still give the audience a feeling of watching the screen
  rather than you.

- ## Techno-failure still possible

  Could be less of a problem if you prepared handouts. In an
  emergency and for very small groups, I've actually held the
  overhead transparency up against a piece of white paper.
  Weak, but it works.

- ## Can cause "retina burns" and vertigo

  Every time you change pages you have this glaring white
  screen to deal with. It gets old after a while. Using a "flipper"
  helps. A flipper is simply a piece of cardboard taped to the top
  of the projector lens. It allows you to first cover the lens, then
  change transparencies, then uncover the lens in a more
  slide-like effect, but this takes time to master. Also,
  less-than-perfect alignment causes page tilting and fumbling
  distractions.

FLIP-CHART or WHITE BOARD

Overwhelmingly my favorite visual format is the flip chart. The
white board or dry-erase board is a close second, but the flip chart is

better because you can refer back to visuals you created earlier in the presentation and you can rip off pages and tape them up to the walls for that "roll-up-your-sleeves" kind of presentation.

Flip Chart: Pros

- ### Very easy & intuitive to use

  It's a breeze and no technology is needed aside from marking pens and tape for a multi-chart presentation.

- ### Low cost

  Buy one for $75 or rent from the facility for $25. Often they won't charge you anything.

- ### Customizable and flexible content

  You can design the visual and make any changes right on the spot.

- ### Allows more dramatic visual technique

  Sweeping lines, circles, bold underlines, exclamation points, stars, the whole world of visual display is at your command. Also you can use "builds" which may be bullet points or charts done one piece at a time. This is a potent technique which generates a very strong understanding.

- ### Makes audience think you are a genius

  This is the big one! When you create the visual right in front of them, they think it's really coming from you. In reality, you may be simply copying something you saw or read that came out of marketing, but they don't know that. This goes a long way to building respect and confidence.

Flip Chart: Cons

- ### Bad penmanship

  Printing large, neat text or drawing clear pictures is not a skill that comes naturally to everyone. Practice helps and you can partially prepare some more complex pages before the seminar.

- ### Looks too home-grown

  Flip charts by definition are not fancy. Color is limited and you can't really draw elaborate pictures. They may not be sufficient for the depth of your presentation.

- ## Can't be seen from back of room

  Flip charts are usually not a viable medium for groups over 50 people. Depending on the layout, they will not be visible in the back or on the sides of the room.

- ## Requires speaker to think

  It's much harder to "put it on auto-pilot" when you're expected to create the visual on a flip chart. Sometimes, a speaker will get lazy and simply avoid the visual.

- ## Back to the audience

  Writing on the chart forces you to take your eyes off the crowd. This allows them to pass notes and throw spitballs. No, seriously...it can be a problem depending on how much you need the visuals to support your talk. Turning away is not always a bad thing, it can actually have some dramatic benefits if used properly, but you should avoid speaking to the chart.

COMPUTER SHOWS

I mentioned earlier that I'm in the process of revising my opinion about computer-generated screen or slide shows. These have many of the advantages and drawbacks of regular film slides plus a few new wrinkles.

Computer: Pros *(beyond those of regular slides)*

- ### Very low cost

  Assuming you already have a laptop computer, the cost of preparing a presentation is the software. You can get PowerPoint or Freelance Graphics for under $200, so this is not a problem for most. I'm not counting the projector!

- ### Very high quality

  Getting the images from your laptop monitor to the screen at the front of the room requires some fancy equipment, but the result is usually excellent. It rivals the best film slides in quality of picture.

- ### Visually exciting

  You can use animation, builds, fade-outs and a whole host of other special effects to enhance your show. These can be distracting, but if done well, they can add to the enjoyment and impact of the presentation.

- # You can build in blank spots

  Remember we said that turning the slide projector off was one of the best presentation techniques you could use. With the computer, you can create blank slides that allow for those "no-visual" moments and call them up on demand with a right mouse click. You could do this with regular slides too, but it's more expensive and impossible to insert them on the fly.

- # Multi-media is still new and fun

  Audiences seem to enjoy the technology and are not yet bored by the medium as they are with slides or overheads. I've done meetings with my laptop and noticed people walk by, turn around and come into the room just because the technology was new and interesting. With sound, animation, and video all blended into a presentation, you're hitting a lot of sensory hot buttons. Naturally, this will wear off over time, but it hasn't yet.

Computer: Cons

- # Techno-failure a major possibility

  Now you've got the space shuttle of presentations going. One of a dozen things can go wrong leaving you in the cold, dark silence of the presentation void. The computer, the software, the connection to the projector, the projector itself...all of it can crash your show with little hope of an elegant recovery.

- # High cost of projectors

  These puppies are a few grand or over $300 to rent. That hurts.

Those are the only drawbacks I can see to computer shows beyond the normal slide problems. Try them for yourself and see how you like them. My guess is that they are going to become the norm.

CHAPTER 20

Call to Action

"No man is worth his salt who is not ready at all times to risk his body...to risk his well-being...to risk his life...in a great cause."
Theodore Roosevelt

This has been fun. I want to thank you for staying with me 'till the end. Like any good seminar, this book must become more than an academic exercise if it is to have any impact on your business. My call to action for you is this:

1. Commit to doing at least one seminar per quarter for the next year. That's four events spaced out with enough preparation time even given a very busy workload.

2. Commit to trying one or two specific techniques you've learned in here. I hope you use them all, but start slowly until you get comfortable. When you see the incredible results, you will want to use more of these skills and speak more frequently. The effect will snowball into a monster business.

3. Commit to having fun. Seminars are a blast!

OK...I've given you my best...the rest is up to you. I'm available to help you in any way at any time! Just call me. Meanwhile, think big, be bold, and as we say on stage...

Break a leg!

Appendix

Appendix #1
Letter To Clubs & Organizations

Mr. Joe Slate
Grand Poobah
The Water Buffalo Lodge
123 Flint Street
Bedrock, USA 12345

Dear Mr. Slate:

As a leader in your organization, one of your jobs may involve arranging for guest speakers on topics of general interest. I would like to offer my help.

I am a practicing expert in the field of investing and personal finance. This is a topic that is on the minds of many people faced with serious questions about their financial future. People are asking:

- How can I make my money work harder and still get the safety I need?
- How can lessen the bite of income tax?
- What types of investments are right for me today?
- How can I plan for my retirement?
- What is going on with this market?

I have prepared a series of entertaining, seminar-style talks on a wide variety of investment related topics. This program is enjoyable, informative and designed to get your people thinking. It is absolutely NOT a sales pitch of any kind!

These seminars are presented solely as educational and social events. They are suitable for both the novice and the experienced investor. They will fit comfortably into your regular meeting agenda — they're fun and they're FREE!

I have enclosed a handful of comments from some recent seminars. I think you'll see that my talks were well-received. Enclosed as well is a **"Topic Menu."** You may select from one of these presentations or we can customize a talk for your group based on their interests.

If you think you might be interested, or would like more information, please return the enclosed information sheet, or contact me directly. My business card is attached.

I look forward to meeting with you and your organization.

Sincerely,

Joe Tentpeg

P.S. If you ever need a last minute replacement for a program, please call me. I will make every effort to help.

Comments from other seminars

"The greatest presentation I've ever heard!"
  D. Trump, New York

"A very interesting and entertaining evening!"
  M. McFly, Mill Valley

"Thanks for the great time. We enjoyed your talk completely!"
  M. Klinger, Toledo

"This was the best seminar we've ever had!"
  Y. A. Tittle, New Jersey

"Superb job! And a very enjoyable evening!"
  Ba Ba Booey, Long Island

"Fantastic job. You gave us a very valuable insight into the world of money. And we had a lot of fun too!"
  J. T. Kirk, Iowa

"A very interesting, funny and enjoyable evening. Please come back!"
  F. Mulder, Washington, DC

NOTE TO THE READER

Don't underestimate the power of these endorsements. A club or organization president runs a big risk when they invite an unknown guest speaker to a meeting. If the members don't enjoy the presentation, the leader is going to catch Hell.

If you can get actual comments from the leaders of other clubs and organizations...it's going to be a much easier process.

Seminar Topic Menu

"22 Ways to Save Money on Income Taxes"
A comprehensive look at 22 tax-saving strategies including: IRAs, Keogh's, 401-k plans, municipal bonds, zero-coupons, tax shelters, gifts to minors, charitable contributions, and much more.

"Global Investing - The Wave of the Future"
A broad overview of growth and income investing overseas. Why foreign markets are expected to outperform the U.S. going forward. The mechanics of investing abroad including a discussion of American Depository Receipts (ADRs), unit trusts and mutual funds. Plus four specific strategies that can be incorporated into any portfolio.

"Growth Investing — The Equity Advantage"
A discussion covering the basics of the stock market...who should be buying stocks and why? We will examine the forces at work in today's market and how they will affect various industry groups. We will compare and contrast Fundamental and Technical Analysis, and show you how the "experts" pick the winners. Plus - *"Maselli's Rules of the Game."*

"Bright Opportunities in Electric Utility Stocks"
An energetic and enlightening look at a group that has become one of the most popular investments in the nation. We will spark some controversy as we shed some light on the myths that have evolved in this industry. Nuclear vs. Non-nuclear, The Regulatory nightmare, and the new tax changes.

"Options and Derivatives as a Strategic Investment"
An examination of the options/derivatives explosion. What are they, and how can they can be used intelligently in volatile markets? We will explore three basic strategies of option/derivative investing: income enhancement, investment hedging, and speculation.

"Modern Portfolio Theory"
Institutional investors have been using it for years...and now it's our turn. Learn how to construct a portfolio that gives you the maximum return for the minimum risk. We will discuss asset allocation, style diversification, the efficient frontier and other money management concepts that can be applied to your portfolio to boost performance right now.

"The Information Highway"
A detailed look at one of the most exciting investment opportunities to come along in many years. Who are the players? We'll examine the four main groups expected to benefit from this trend: Technology Enablers, Transporters, Content Providers and Users. Plus - How to invest.

Personal Financial Planning:

Part 1 - "Getting Started"

We will discuss the basics of financial planning and how you can use it to first identify and then meet your specific goals. We will examine the planning process from the Income Statement through the Personal Balance Sheet. We will explore the principles of Liquidity, Leverage, and Diversification.

Part 2 - "Selecting the Investments that are Right for You"

A general overview of the investment world with a more specific focus on various programs and investment vehicles designed to meet individual needs. We will examine strategies for maximizing growth, income, and tax advantages. A look at the pros and cons of stocks, bonds, Government Securities, municipal bonds, annuities, real estate, options, and mutual funds.

NOTE TO THE READER

This menu of courses can be tailored to fit your specific areas of specialization. You might include estate planning, insurance, whatever your heart desires.

Some of the courses I've listed are there for a reason. For example, I don't expect anyone to request the Options & Derivatives course. I've listed it as a "positioning element." I've said that I'm an "expert" in the field of investing and this is one of those highly technical subjects that no one understands...except me. Get the idea?

If you're going to get serious about marketing yourself for these kinds of seminars, you're going to want your materials to look professional. You might consider having your letter, topic menu and endorsements combined into a four-page brochure that includes a mail-reply card.

Appendix 2

Customized Note Paper

This should be handed out or pre-set for each attendee. As a minimum, it should contain the title of the seminar, date, your name and phone number. You can get very elaborate with notes and handouts, but simplicity is often the best course of action.

Avoiding the Retirement Nightmare
Jan 15, 1997
with
Joe Tentpeg of Blowhard & Boggle
800-734-9378

NOTES

Appendix #3
The Storyboard Workbook

This is a fairly elaborate handout item that you can use for higher-end presentations.

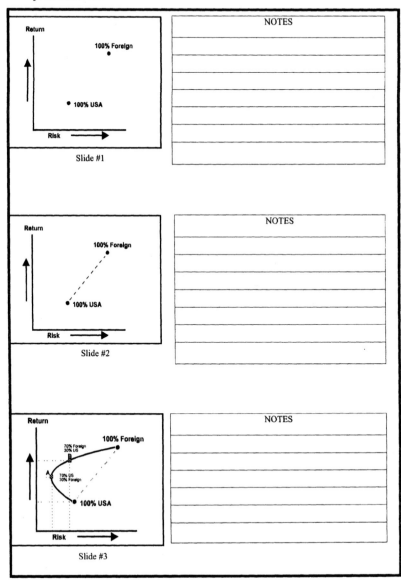

Appendix #5

Five Week Seminar Planner

Week 5

- Choose date, time, and topic of seminar (Check for conflicts or holidays)
- Book the location
- Order hand-out materials (i.e., brochures, research reports)
- Call advertising and order ad slicks or mail invitations
- Notify manager and request needed support
- Begin script outline
- Design seminar invitation
- Contact all free sources of advertising (i.e., church bulletins, Community Calendar of Events section, radio and cable TV bulletin boards, etc.)
- Begin developing your storybook (research, gather data, articles etc.)

Week 4

- Deadline for major changes (date, time location or topic)
- Finalize script outline and submit for Compliance approval as needed
- Double-check date and time for conflicts
- Follow-up on support request from management as needed
- Gather list of prospects to invite
- Finalize invitation design and take to the printer
- Notify assistants of upcoming workload or projected overtime
- Plan for projected postage needs

Week 3

- Start addressing invitations
- Ship bulk mail 20-18 days prior to seminar
- Make final changes in script outline
- Follow-up with advertising to insure proper placement of ads
- Begin to notify clients and ask them to bring a friend

Week 2

- Ship first class mail no later than 14 days prior to seminar
- Begin calling your invitation list
- Practice your presentation and memorize appropriate sections
- Inspect hand-out materials and visuals

Week 1

- Continue calling to invite
- Put together hand-out kits
- Double check placement of ads and any appearances of free advertising
- Have assistant prepare sign-up sheet
- Videotape and review your "dress rehearsal" presentation
- Finalize head count with the facility (72 hours prior with final count 24 hours)
- Call to confirm attendees the day of the seminar or prior day for an AM event
- Scan all news media for hot stories the audience might see

Appendix #6
Seminar Questionnaire
(front page)

This can be handed out at the beginning of the event and collected at the end. As follow-up to the seminar, you should offer some item of value, such as a portfolio review, and have them request this in the "Comments" section on the back page before they turn in the sheet. This "freebie" will cause most people to turn in a profile and you will be amazed by all the information you get.

Confidential Seminar Profile & Comment Sheet

Name _____   Home Phone_____

Address _____   Work Phone _____

_____

Your age _____   Your occupation or title _____

Your company or employer _____ # Years there _____

Your planned retirement age _____ Do you have a 401(k)? _____

Spouse's Name _____ Age _____

Occupation/Title _____

Spouse's employer _____ # Years there _____

Spouse's retirement plan type _____

How many children? _____ Ages _____

ANNUAL INCOME RANGE
- ☐ $25,000 - $75,000
- ☐ $75,000 - $150,000
- ☐ $150,000 - $350,000
- ☐ Over $355,000

NET WORTH RANGE
- ☐ $50,000 - $100,000
- ☐ $100,000 - $600,000
- ☐ $600,000 - $1.2 million
- ☐ Over $1.2 million

Investment Objectives (Please rank the following in order of importance 1=HIGH, 9=LOW)

- ☐ Saving for retirement
- ☐ Reducing taxes
- ☐ Increasing income
- ☐ Growing my asset base
- ☐ College funding
- ☐ Safety of principal
- ☐ Speculative growth
- ☐ Inflation protection
- ☐ Other _____

I am currently investing in: (Please check all that apply)

- ☐ Stocks (list major holdings _____
- ☐ Bonds (which type? _____
- ☐ Mutual funds (which?)_____
- ☐ Annuities / Insurance
- ☐ Partnerships
- ☐ Foreign investments
- ☐ Commodities
- ☐ Certificates of deposit

I would like to learn more about: (Please check all that apply)

- ☐ Retirement planning
- ☐ Growth investments
- ☐ Income investments
- ☐ Tax-free bonds
- ☐ U.S. Government securities
- ☐ Foreign/Global investments
- ☐ Estate planning
- ☐ Modern Portfolio Theory
- ☐ asset allocation
- ☐ reducing my risk exposure
- ☐ "Mid-cap" stocks
- ☐ "Micro-cap" stocks

Seminar Questionnaire
(back page)

This is the flip side of the Seminar Questionnaire. The comments are very simple and straightforward. Naturally, this can be tailored to fit your needs, but the basic premise is to make it very easy for them to provide feedback.

You may want to review this with the audience during the recap portion of the seminar or have an assistant do it after you've done the close.

Seminar Critique & Comments (Your comments are very important to us!)

	YES!		Neutral		NO!
I found the overall seminar to be valuable.	5	4	3	2	1
The topic was interesting.	5	4	3	2	1
Frank was well prepared.	5	4	3	2	1
The visuals were easy to read.	5	4	3	2	1
Frank's presentation held my interest.	5	4	3	2	1
I found most points very understandable.	5	4	3	2	1
The room was comfortable.	5	4	3	2	1
The food was good.	5	4	3	2	1
I would come to another seminar.	5	4	3	2	1
I would tell a friend about these seminars.	5	4	3	2	1

Comments:

_____

_____

_____

_____

Thank you very much for your comments. They will help us improve our service in the future.

Index

Index

About the Author

Frank Maselli brings a unique combination of business and theatrical experiences to the subject of investment seminars. He graduated from Lafayette College in 1978 with a degree in Biology. He then served five years as an Army officer stationed at Fort Meade, Maryland, where he commanded a modern M*A*S*H* hospital.

Frank began his investment career in 1983 with Dean Witter Reynolds in Baltimore. The experience of being at a Sears Financial Center convinced him early on of the tremendous value in face-to-face client contact and led him to seminars as his primary business-building tool.

He joined PaineWebber in 1986 and served for ten years in a variety of sales and managerial roles all the while continuing his seminar effort. As a Regional Sales Director for Mutual Funds, he conducted hundreds of seminars throughout the nation and trained hundreds of Investment Executives in advanced presentation techniques.

Frank's first stage appearance came at age fourteen and led to a continuous relationship with the theater that has seen him with leading roles in over 100 productions ranging from Shakespeare to musical comedy. He studied acting with Don McBee in Baltimore.

Frank is presently Senior Vice President and National Sales Manager for New England Funds in Boston. He travels the country speaking to groups about the funds and about seminars and has become one of the most sought-after speakers in the industry.

Frank is a member of MENSA, The Planetary Society and a private pilot. He enjoys golf, boating and trap shooting with his wife Rebecca.